An Analysis of

John Stuart Mill's

Utilitarianism

Patrick Tom
with
Sander Werkhoven

www.macat.com
info@macat.com

Cover illustration: Etienne Gilfillan

Cataloguing in Publication Data
A catalogue record for this book is available from the British Library.
Library of Congress Cataloguing-in-Publication Data is available upon request.

ISBN 978-1-912303-39-7 (hardback)
ISBN 978-1-912127-83-2 (paperback)
ISBN 978-1-912282-27-2 (e-book)

Notice
The information in this book is designed to orientate readers of the work under analysis,
to elucidate and contextualise its key ideas and themes, and to aid in the development
of critical thinking skills. It is not meant to be used, nor should it be used, as a
substitute for original thinking or in place of original writing or research. References and
notes are provided for informational purposes and their presence does not constitute
endorsement of the information or opinions therein. This book is presented solely for
educational purposes. It is sold on the understanding that the publisher is not engaged
to provide any scholarly advice. The publisher has made every effort to ensure that
this book is accurate and up-to-date, but makes no warranties or representations with
regard to the completeness or reliability of the information it contains. The information
and the opinions provided herein are not guaranteed or warranted to produce particular
results and may not be suitable for students of every ability. The publisher shall not be
liable for any loss, damage or disruption arising from any errors or omissions, or from
the use of this book, including, but not limited to, special, incidental, consequential or
other damages caused, or alleged to have been caused, directly or indirectly, by the
information contained within.

CONTENTS

THE MACAT LIBRARY

The Macat Library is a series of unique academic explorations of seminal works in the humanities and social sciences – books and papers that have had a significant and widely recognised impact on their disciplines. It has been created to serve as much more than just a summary of what lies between the covers of a great book. It illuminates and explores the influences on, ideas of, and impact of that book. Our goal is to offer a learning resource that encourages critical thinking and fosters a better, deeper understanding of important ideas.

Each publication is divided into three Sections: Influences, Ideas, and Impact. Each Section has four Modules. These explore every important facet of the work, and the responses to it.

This Section-Module structure makes a Macat Library book easy to use, but it has another important feature. Because each Macat book is written to the same format, it is possible (and encouraged!) to cross-reference multiple Macat books along the same lines of inquiry or research. This allows the reader to open up interesting interdisciplinary pathways.

To further aid your reading, lists of glossary terms and people mentioned are included at the end of this book (these are indicated by an asterisk [*] throughout) – as well as a list of works cited.

Macat has worked with the University of Cambridge to identify the elements of critical thinking and understand the ways in which six different skills combine to enable effective thinking.
Three allow us to fully understand a problem; three more give us the tools to solve it. Together, these six skills make up the **PACIER** model of critical thinking. They are:

ANALYSIS – understanding how an argument is built
EVALUATION – exploring the strengths and weaknesses of an argument
INTERPRETATION – understanding issues of meaning

CREATIVE THINKING – coming up with new ideas and fresh connections
PROBLEM-SOLVING – producing strong solutions
REASONING – creating strong arguments

To find out more, visit **WWW.MACAT.COM.**

CRITICAL THINKING AND *UTILITARIANISM*

Primary critical thinking skill: REASONING
Secondary critical thinking skill: INTERPRETATION

John Stuart Mill's 1861 *Utilitarianism* remains one of the most widely known and influential works of moral philosophy ever written. It is also a model of critical thinking – one in which Mill's reasoning and interpretation skills are used to create a well-structured, watertight, persuasive argument for his position on core questions in ethics.

The central question, for Mill, was to decide upon a valid definition of right and wrong, and reason out his moral theory from there. Laying down valid, defensible definitions is a crucial aspect of good interpretative thinking, and Mill gets his in as early as possible. Actions are good, he suggests, if they increase happiness, and bad if they reduce happiness. But, vitally, it is not our own happiness that matters, but the total happiness of all those affected by a given action. From this interpretation of moral good, Mill is able to systematically reason out a coherent framework for calculating and judging overall happiness, while considering different kinds and qualities of happiness.

Like any good example of reasoning, Mill's argument consistently takes account of possible objections, building them into the structure of the book in order to acknowledge and counter them as he goes.

ABOUT THE AUTHOR OF THE ORIGINAL WORK

Son of the Scottish philosopher **James Mill**, the philosopher and economist John Stuart Mill was a child prodigy who learned Greek at three, Latin at eight, and was studying political economy at 13. Unsurprisingly, he suffered a nervous breakdown at 20, but recovered to continue working for the East India Company – Britain's proxy government in India – and later become a Liberal Member of Parliament. Mill was one of the first people to demand the right to vote for women. He backed a number of social reforms, and helped define concepts of freedom in his writing. He died in 1873 in France.

ABOUT THE AUTHORS OF THE ANALYSIS

Dr Patrick Tom holds masters degrees from Notre Dame, Leeds and the University of Zimbabwe, and a PhD in politics and international relations from the University of St Andrews. He currently works for the Zimbabwe Policy Dialogue Institute.

Dr Sander Werkhoven holds a PhD in philosophy from the University of Warwick. He is currently a member of the Department of Philosophy and Religious Studies at the University of Utrecht, where he specialises in ethics and the philosophy of medicine.

ABOUT MACAT

GREAT WORKS FOR CRITICAL THINKING

Macat is focused on making the ideas of the world's great thinkers accessible and comprehensible to everybody, everywhere, in ways that promote the development of enhanced critical thinking skills.

It works with leading academics from the world's top universities to produce new analyses that focus on the ideas and the impact of the most influential works ever written across a wide variety of academic disciplines. Each of the works that sit at the heart of its growing library is an enduring example of great thinking. But by setting them in context – and looking at the influences that shaped their authors, as well as the responses they provoked – Macat encourages readers to look at these classics and game-changers with fresh eyes. Readers learn to think, engage and challenge their ideas, rather than simply accepting them.

"Macat offers an amazing first-of-its-kind tool for interdisciplinary learning and research. Its focus on works that transformed their disciplines and its rigorous approach, drawing on the world's leading experts and educational institutions, opens up a world-class education to anyone."

Andreas Schleicher
Director for Education and Skills, Organisation for Economic Co-operation and Development

'Macat is taking on some of the major challenges in university education ... They have drawn together a strong team of active academics who are producing teaching materials that are novel in the breadth of their approach.'

Prof Lord Broers,
former Vice-Chancellor of the University of Cambridge

'The Macat vision is exceptionally exciting. It focuses upon new modes of learning which analyse and explain seminal texts which have profoundly influenced world thinking and so social and economic development. It promotes the kind of critical thinking which is essential for any society and economy. This is the learning of the future.'

Rt Hon Charles Clarke, former UK Secretary of State for Education

'The Macat analyses provide immediate access to the critical conversation surrounding the books that have shaped their respective discipline, which will make them an invaluable resource to all of those, students and teachers, working in the field.'

Professor William Tronzo, University of California at San Diego

WAYS IN TO THE TEXT

KEY POINTS

- John Stuart Mill (1806–73) was a British philosopher, political activist, and Member of Parliament. A defender of individual liberty throughout his writings and political career, he developed the moral philosophy of utilitarianism.

- According to his work *Utilitarianism* (1861), happiness, the greatest good in human life, is produced by morally good action.

- *Utilitarianism* is a key text in moral philosophy—the branch of philosophy that inquires into ethics. It clearly explains the utilitarian doctrine and defends it against objections.

Who Was John Stuart Mill?

John Stuart Mill, the author of *Utilitarianism* (1861), was a British philosopher, economist, and civil servant. Born in 1806, he was the son of James Mill,* a Scottish philosopher and historian, and his wife, Harriet Burrow. James Mill taught his son from an early age about ancient philosophy and the moral theory of utilitarianism. In this he was helped by the philosopher and jurist* (legal scholar) Jeremy Bentham,* generally considered to be the founder of utilitarianism. Both men hoped that the young John Stuart Mill would himself become a believer in utilitarianism and carry on the tradition. He did.

Mill, a political activist and important social reformer, wrote many essays and philosophical works over his lifetime. His first major published text was *A System of Logic* (1843), in which he argues in favor of logic as a method of proof. In 1848, he published *Principles of Political Economy*, a major text in nineteenth-century economic theory. His 1859 essay *On Liberty* offers a defense of individual liberty and argues that conduct that causes harm to others should be limited. In 1863 he published *Utilitarianism*, in which he explains and defends the moral theory of his tutor, Jeremy Bentham.

Active at a time of major social change in Britain, Mill was well known in his own lifetime. For three years he was a Member of Parliament for the Liberal Party,* a British political party with policies founded on belief in the importance of individual liberty; during this period, he campaigned to give women the right to vote. Mill married the philosopher and campaigner Harriet Taylor* in 1851 after two decades of friendship. A great thinker in her own right, she helped Mill to develop his philosophical, economic, and political theories.

What Does *Utilitarianism* Say?

Utilitarianism is a book dealing with moral philosophy, particularly the question of how we should act and how we should live our lives. In it, Mill argues that happiness is the goal of human life, and that things can only be considered as "good" if they promote human happiness. Mill thinks this first argument can be empirically* proven (that is, proven by making deductions from observable evidence); human beings, he points out, do in fact all try to attain happiness. He defines "happiness" as the experience of pleasure and the absence of pain and suffering (a definition that might be understood as "hedonistic").* The goal of human life is, therefore, the experience of pleasure and the absence of pain and suffering; this is also the ultimate good.

Although he takes this idea from his tutor and predecessor Jeremy Bentham, Mill points out that the idea was also present in the ethical works of the Ancient Greeks, especially the philosopher Epicurus.* He builds on this long tradition by distinguishing between higher and lower pleasures, recognizing that not all pleasures are equally relevant in terms of measures of happiness; in assessing happiness, he argues, more importance has to be given to higher pleasures, such as those we take from poetry, music, and the development of insight.

From the belief that happiness is the ultimate goal of human life, Mill then derives the most important thesis of the book—namely, that an action is morally good if it increases happiness and reduces suffering, and morally bad if it does the opposite. Importantly, it is not one's own happiness that morally good action promotes, but the total happiness of all those affected by one's actions. Mill writes that "the foundation of morals, Utility, or the Greatest Happiness Principle* ... holds that actions are right in proportion as they tend to promote happiness, wrong as they tend to produce the reverse of happiness."[1] This, in short, is the principle of utility.*

In *Utilitarianism* Mill defends this moral theory, even if it implies that one's own happiness might have to be sacrificed, and addresses many criticisms that his contemporaries raised against the principle of utility. Of these, the objection that it conflicts with our sense of justice is especially notable. In the final part of the book Mill discusses the relationship between justice and utility, arguing that justice is also based upon the principle of utility, and that therefore no conflict exists between what is just and what is morally right.

Why Does *Utilitarianism* Matter?

Utilitarianism is a key text in the history of philosophy. Its systematic and detailed defense of utilitarianism led to the principle becoming one of the three most important moral theories in Western philosophy.

Mill placed great emphasis on good moral education. His text, aimed at a general audience, aims to teach us how to think about moral questions in order to make us all better and happier people. We all wonder how we should act in some given situation, and we often ask ourselves, "What is the right thing to do here?" Mill's utilitarianism gives us an answer. The right thing to do, he writes, is the thing that brings about the *most* happiness and the *least* unhappiness. This is a far more practical principle than most other moral theories offered, and his defense of this idea might well lead to many of his readers thinking differently about the right way to act.

Utilitarianism is more than just an educational text, however; a foundational text of the utilitarian tradition, it both clearly defines and defends utilitarian principles. In Mill's time, many believed that utilitarianism was inadequate as a moral philosophy. But Mill's strong, comprehensive, and very intelligent defense helped utilitarianism become one of the most important theories in moral philosophy in the twentieth century. Despite the fact that many different strands of utilitarianism have been developed since Mill's time, they all build on Mill's insights and their arguments are backed up by this text.

Utilitarianism is therefore not only a founding text of one of the most important theories in moral philosophy—it continues to be highly relevant in debates about how we ought to act, and how we should live our lives.

NOTES

1   John Stuart Mill, *Utilitarianism*, ed. Roger Crisp (Oxford: Oxford University Press, 1998), 55.

SECTION 1
INFLUENCES

MODULE 1
THE AUTHOR AND THE HISTORICAL CONTEXT

KEY POINTS

- Mill's *Utilitarianism* is a founding text in the history of moral philosophy (the philosophical consideration of ethics). It developed the English social reformer and philosopher Jeremy Bentham's* utilitarian views into a refined and comprehensive moral theory.

- Mill was brought up to become a strong promoter of utilitarianism. Jeremy Bentham himself played a large part in his education.

- Mill wrote at a time of social and political change and responded to it by supporting liberalism* (a social movement founded to promote and defend individual liberty).

Why Read This Text?

John Stuart Mill, the author of *Utilitarianism* (1861), is one of the most influential thinkers and liberal reformers of the nineteenth century. The work, among his most widely read philosophical works, offers a definition and philosophical defense of the ethical theory* of utilitarianism, modifying and expanding the work of previous utilitarian theorists.

An "ethical theory" is a reasoned account of how humans ought to behave or act; according to utilitarian principles, we should promote the good (where good means more overall happiness than unhappiness). Although it is a theory associated with John Stuart Mill and the British philosopher and jurist Jeremy Bentham, its core ideas did not originate with them.

❝ I went through the whole process of preparing my Greek lessons in the same room and at the same table at which [my father] was writing ... I was forced to have recourse to him for the meaning of every word which I did not know. This incessant interruption, he, one of the most impatient of men, submitted to, and wrote under that interruption several volumes of his History and all else that he had to write during those years. ❞

John Stuart Mill, *Autobiography*

Mill's *Utilitarianism*, in which we find a fully worked-out version of utilitarianism, still serves as one of the most important texts in moral philosophy. In it, Mill distinguishes between higher pleasures—poetry and the development of insight, for example—and lower pleasures, arguing that the former are more important in the total sum of happiness. At the heart of the utilitarian belief system he places human sympathy rather than the "greatest happiness principle"* put forward by his teacher Bentham (the latter being an idea more calculative*— that is, determined through calculation—in nature). Mill also argues at great length why we should act according to utilitarian morality.

With these modifications and expansions, Mill tries to defend utilitarianism against a number of objections that continue to be raised in literature on the subject today. The continuing interest in Mill's *Utilitarianism* is therefore not only due to its founding role in moral philosophy; the text also provides powerful answers to objections that are still made against utilitarianism.

Author's Life
Mill was born in London in 1806 and died in 1873. His father, James Mill,* agreed with the teachings of the seventeenth-century

English philosopher John Locke,* who claimed that the human mind is a *tabula rasa**—a blank slate—at birth and that knowledge is acquired through experience. Wanting his son to continue the utilitarian political and social reform program after he and his friend Jeremy Bentham had died, James Mill embarked on a rigorous program of education in which he personally tutored his son in order to produce the perfect utilitarian mind.[1] In his autobiography, John Stuart Mill records how his father told him to study Greek and Latin, and made him systematically go through all the classical texts.

Mill records in his autobiography that he was required to study Ancient Greek "in the same room and at the same table" at which his father worked;"I was forced to have recourse to him," he wrote, "for the meaning of every word which I did not know."[2]

But this education did not immediately have the desired effect. In 1826, Mill suffered a severe mental crisis; his eventual recovery came through his engagement with poetry, and in particular with the work of the English poets William Wordsworth* and Samuel Taylor Coleridge,* which was typical of the Romantic* tradition in its emotionally oriented and descriptive qualities. Mill hoped to develop his aesthetic sensibilities by reading these poems.[3]

Following his recovery, he started to shape his own philosophical views. He emphasized the importance of emotions and feelings in human life and, in doing so, distanced his thought from the more calculative aspects of Bentham's utilitarianism.[4] Nevertheless, Mill remained committed to utilitarianism and empiricism* (the belief that knowledge should be based on experience) until the end of his life. In his autobiography, Mill credits his wife, Harriet Taylor Mill,* with helping him develop his philosophical thought.

Mill was also a political activist and served in parliament from 1865 to 1868 as a member of the Liberal Party. He was the first British parliamentarian to support the right of women to vote, and was a passionate and lifelong supporter of that cause.

Author's Background

Mill lived in a period when Britain was experiencing substantial social and economic changes as a result of the country's move from an economy based on agriculture and manual labor to one based on industrial production. This period, called the Industrial Revolution,* led to economic growth in Britain, but also resulted in a number of challenges, including an increase in inequality, rapid urbanization, unemployment, crime, rising prices, a massive rise in poverty, declining wages, poor housing, and a surge in illnesses. The nineteenth century was dominated by campaigns and debates on political reform (in part, inspired by the French Revolution* of 1789 to 1799, in the course of which the French king was executed and the government was radically reformed). There were loud demands for individual freedom, for democratic and parliamentary reforms, for a minimal state, for a free-enterprise economy, and for the need to establish a more tolerant and fairer society. During this period, there were also calls for the replacement of aristocratic rule with a representative government. In nineteenth-century Britain, the liberal political movement was opposed to aristocratic rule, its members believing that Parliament comprised a corrupt elite who acted in their own interests and violated individual liberty.

In short, Mill lived during a period of social upheaval. These challenges inspired much of his work and philosophical activity. He reacted to the changing conditions and advocated liberalism.

NOTES

1 John Stuart Mill, *Autobiography*, ed. Jack Stillinger (London: Oxford University Press, 1971).

2 Mill, *Autobiography*, 9.

3 See Mill, *Autobiography*; Thomas Woods, *Poetry and Philosophy: A Study in the Thought of John Stuart Mill* (London: Hutchinson & Co., 1961).

4 See John Stuart Mill, "Bentham," in *Utilitarianism and Other Essays*, ed. Alan Ryan (London: Penguin Books, 2004).

MODULE 2
ACADEMIC CONTEXT

KEY POINTS

- *Utilitarianism* is a work in moral philosophy, offering an answer to the question how one ought to live.

- In it, Mill offers an alternative theory to classical virtue ethics* (an approach to understanding "right" action, dating to Ancient Greece, that focuses on the individual's cultivation of virtuous behavior) and deontology* (an approach to ethics founded on notions of duty and moral obligation* that owes much to the eighteenth-century German philosopher Immanuel Kant*).

- Although Mill was heavily influenced by his father and the Utilitarian philosopher Jeremy Bentham,* he also drew from the insights of other philosophers, both ancient and modern, and from contemporary critics of utilitarianism.

The Work in its Context

John Stuart Mill's *Utilitarianism* is a work in the field of moral philosophy, the area of philosophy concerned with the question "How should one live?"

This question, notably raised by the Ancient Greek philosopher Socrates,* can be split into three further questions: "What is happiness?," "How can we know what is morally right?", and "How are we motivated to do the morally right thing?"

Moral philosophy is concerned not with how things *are* in the world, but with how things *should be*. Rather than describing how people make their decisions and go about living their lives or analyzing how societies work, moral philosophy questions how people *should be*

> **❝** In the present work I shall, without further discussion of the other theories, try to contribute something towards the understanding and appreciation of the Utilitarian or Happiness theory, and towards such proof as it can be given. **❞**
>
> John Stuart Mill, *Utilitarianism*

living their life, and how society *should be* organized. There has long been skepticism about the possibility of finding answers to questions in moral philosophy. Many believe that it is up to an individual to decide how they live their life. Most moral philosophers, however, argue that there is such a thing as a right action and a wrong action, a morally better or worse person, and more or less just ways of social organization. Mill's *Utilitarianism* presents an argument for one such view.

Overview of the Field

Generally, there are three traditions in moral philosophy: virtue ethics, Kantian deontology, and utilitarianism.

Virtue ethics is usually associated with the work of the Greek philosopher Aristotle,* the student of the enormously influential thinker Plato.*[1] In Aristotle's view, what determines the nature of human beings is their capacity to reason. To live a good life we must exercise our capacity to reason *well* (that is, to reason in accordance with "excellence"). In Aristotle's view, it is the "virtuous agent" (in other words, a person making excellent use of his or her capacity to reason) who will know how to act in specific circumstances. Rather than being a general principle determining what is right and wrong, the virtue ethical position is that well-educated and virtuous agents will reliably choose the best course of action.

Kantian deontology, developed by the greatly influential German philosopher Immanuel Kant, by contrast, looks not at the character traits of the individual, but at the rightness and the wrongness of an action itself.[2] Kant tried to formulate a universal principle on the basis of "pure reason," paying no attention to what makes people happy. Kant's view is that morally good action consists in acting in accordance with a principle that one should be able to rationally *will* (that is, rationally_want to come about) as a universal law.

So if one can rationally will a principle of action as a universal law, the action is morally good; if one cannot rationally will it (that is, if it were to result in contradictions), the action is morally wrong. This moral test is not about wanting to live in a world where everyone acts on certain principles. It is not the consequences that matter for Kant. What matters is that it must rationally be conceivable that the principle can become a universal law; if it ends up in a contradiction, any action based on the principle is morally wrong.

According to *Utilitarianism*, however, the goodness of an action does not depend on the character of the individual (as in virtue ethics); nor does it depend on the possibility of rationally willing it as a universal law (as in Kantian deontology). Instead, utilitarianism is the view that the goodness of an action depends on its *consequences*. If an action has good consequences, the action is morally good, whether or not it is performed by a virtuous individual. Utilitarians are only interested in the amount of overall happiness and unhappiness an action brings about. The morally right way to act, according to utilitarians, is the way that brings about the most good: it must increase the total amount of happiness in the world and decrease the total amount of unhappiness.

Academic Influences

The most direct influences on Mill's thinking were his father, James Mill,* and his tutor, the "founder" of modern utilitarianism, Jeremy Bentham. They were both part of the intellectual tradition known as "philosophical radicals,*" which also included writers such as the British economic theorist David Ricardo.* But the intellectual world of Mill's youth "combined openness to radicalism in the form of Jeremy Bentham's … with a suspicion bred by his contact with ancients that not every idea of the good is reducible to gross pleasures."[3]

Thus, Mill's thought was also influenced by Ancient Greek philosophy. The idea that happiness is the ultimate purpose of human life, for example, was also present in the writings of ancient philosophers such as Aristotle,* Epicurus,* Aristippus,* and Plato.* The doctrine of utility had long been accepted by thinkers both before and during Mill's time; thinkers such as Claude Adrien Helvétius,* Cesare Beccaria,* John Locke,* David Hume,* and Francis Hutcheson* had all drawn on it to form ideas.

Opponents of utilitarianism included thinkers such as the Scottish philosopher, mathematician, and social commentator Thomas Carlyle* and the English thinker John Ruskin.* Such critics did not view utilitarianism as the "fundamental principle of morality, and the source of moral obligation."*[4] They believed it conflicted with what is actually morally right. Carlyle even claimed that utilitarianism, with its sole focus on pleasure, was in fact a "pig philosophy." Mill's arguments were influenced by these critical voices.

In *Utilitarianism,* Mill brings together the ideas of his father James Mill, his tutor Bentham, the insights offered by the ancient schools of philosophy, and arguments made by critics of utilitarian ideas.

NOTES

1   See Aristotle, *Nicomachean Ethics*, in *The Complete Works of Aristotle, The Revised Oxford Translation*, ed. Jonathan Barnes (Princeton, NJ: Princeton University Press, 1995).

2   For Kant's moral philosophy, see Immanuel Kant, *Groundwork of the Metaphysics of Morals, e*d. and trans. Mary J. Gregor (Cambridge: Cambridge University Press, [1785] 1998).

3   Robert Devigne, *Reforming Liberalism: J. S. Mill's use of Ancient, Religious, Liberal, and Romantic Moralities* (New Haven, CT: Yale University Press, 2006), 2.

4   John Stuart Mill, *Utilitarianism*, ed. Roger Crisp (Oxford: Oxford University Press, 1998), 51.

MODULE 3
THE PROBLEM

KEY POINTS

- Mill's *Utilitarianism* attempts to answer the fundamental moral question of how to live and act by defending and expanding the philosopher Jeremy Bentham's* philosophy of utilitarianism.

- Mill engages with all schools of moral philosophy in Utilitarianism—especially with those authors who raised objections to Bentham's views.

- Mill examined what utilitarianism stood for, how it could be defended against its critics, and why it could be supported by empirical* evidence better than other schools of ethics founded more on intuition.

Core Question

John Stuart Mill's *Utilitarianism* is primarily aimed at answering the question, "What is the right way to act or to live?

In order to answer this question, Mill addresses a series of further questions central to moral philosophy. He asks, first of all, what the "end" or "goal" is of good action. Whenever we think of something as good, we do so because it results in something that we also think of as good. For instance: receiving a high grade at school is good because it might lead to graduate school, which is good because it helps the development of one's intellect, which is good for some further reason—and so on.

At some point this chain has to stop; there must be a *final* good (that is, something which means that everything that has contributed to it is good). Without a final good, we would not know what makes

> ❝ From the dawn of philosophy, the question concerning the [highest good], or, what is the same thing, concerning the foundation of morality, has been accounted the main problem in speculative thought, has occupied the most gifted intellects, and divided them into sects and schools, carrying on a vigorous warfare against one another. And after more than two thousand years the same discussions continue. ❞
>
> John Stuart Mill, *Utilitarianism*

all the other things good. In order to know how to act, Mill thinks we should ask the question, "What does this final good consist of?"

Mill's answer to this question is happiness. But this in turn creates further questions. What does happiness consist of? What is the relationship between happiness and morality? What are we morally obliged to do if the final good is happiness? If happiness is the final good, what is the relationship between happiness and justice? These are the questions that concern Mill in *Utilitarianism*, and which he attempts to answer.

Mill contributes to the philosophical debate on how to act and live. It is the same debate that philosophers such as the Ancient Greek thinkers Plato,* Aristotle,* and Epicurus* and the eighteenth-century German philosopher Immanuel Kant* grappled with. The core questions of Mill's work are no different from earlier philosophical inquiry.

The Participants

In chapter 1 of *Utilitarianism*, Mill states that the followers of the "inductive school of ethics"* and the "intuitive school of ethics"* were in agreement that morality was based on the establishment of principles. The main participants Mill had in mind while writing the text, therefore, were defenders of these two schools. Although both schools agreed that morality required principles, they disagreed about the ultimate source of moral obligation* (that is, action that one has a moral duty to perform). In Jeremy Bentham's version of utilitarianism, pleasure and pain are the only things that govern human behavior, and the principle of utility* (or the greatest happiness principle)* is the basis of morality.[1] Followers of the intuitive school disagreed with this.

Mill also tries to combine the ideas of his father, James Mill, and Jeremy Bentham with those of other thinkers, including Thomas Carlyle* (a Scottish philosopher associated with the literary, artistic, and philosophical movement of Romanticism),* ancient philosophers such as Socrates* and Epicurus, and those such as the French social theorist Auguste Comte,* who subscribed to the tenets of positivism* with their belief that scientific knowledge must be derived from sensory experience and tested by means of experiments. The influence of Comte's positivism is clearly visible in Mill's work, as Mill sees the natural sciences as the only way to gain knowledge. Mill rejects the view held by thinkers such as the German philosopher Immanuel Kant and the British theologian and philosopher William Whewell* that *a priori* ethical principles—that is, ethical principles that can be deduced independently of experience—exist.

The Contemporary Debate

Although the contemporary debate was influenced by supporters of the inductive and intuitive schools of ethics, Mill thought there was also a great deal of misunderstanding about utilitarianism. As well as debates about whether utilitarianism was the *right* moral theory, there was also much discussion about what utilitarianism stood for in the first place. Mill addresses those who think that the promotion of utility in society means *not* promoting happiness. He points out that this is precisely what utilitarianism is about.

A second debate in Mill's time was whether utilitarianism was a kind of "pig philosophy," as Thomas Carlyle described it. Carlyle's critique was specifically aimed at Bentham's utilitarianism. Bentham believed that utility (or happiness) could be measured by adding up all the pleasures that people would experience. Critics argued that this form of utilitarianism was an animalistic moral theory, as it promoted the kind of gross pleasures that govern the actions of animals. Mill defends utilitarianism by arguing (against Bentham) that the *quality* of pleasures is of crucial importance; some pleasures are of a higher quality—and therefore of higher value—than others. This is contrary to Bentham's argument that pleasures that are equivalent in terms of intensity, duration, and certainty have equal value.

Mill also criticizes ethical intuitionism*—the doctrine that we have *a priori* knowledge of moral truths—as he sees it as just reflecting the status quo. He defends utilitarianism on an empirical* basis, saying that experience shows us people do in fact try to act in ways that promote their happiness, especially the kind of happiness that results from the "higher" pleasures.

NOTES

1   Jeremy Bentham, *An Introduction to the Principles of Morals and Legislation*, eds. J. H. Burns and H. L. A. Hurt (London: Athlone, 1970).

MODULE 4
THE AUTHOR'S CONTRIBUTION

KEY POINTS

- In *Utilitarianism*, Mill tries to define the philosophy of utilitarianism and defend it against a number of criticisms, including the criticism that utility means something other than pleasure and happiness.

- *Utilitarianism* takes an empirical* approach to moral philosophy: in it, Mill claims that we can deduce that happiness is the greatest good by observing that we all clearly desire happiness for ourselves.

- Mill defends the greatest happiness principle* put forward by the philosopher Jeremy Bentham, but adds quality of pleasures to the measures of happiness.

Author's Aims

John Stuart Mill points out in the opening passages of *Utilitarianism* that critics of utilitarianism had grossly misunderstood its central doctrine. He goes on to list the many criticisms that had been leveled against utilitarianism: that happiness is actually unattainable; that everyone would end up dissatisfied if they acted on the "greatest happiness principle"; that utilitarian theory relies solely on cold calculation; that total happiness is too complex to calculate; that it is bound to result in conflicting duties; that it leaves no place for God in morality; that it just acts as a kind of self-justification of one's actions; that utilitarianism is a moral theory more suitable to animals than to human beings; and finally, that it conflicts with common ideas about justice.

But the first criticism Mill addresses in chapter 2 of *Utilitarianism* is the criticism that utilitarianism focuses on utility rather than

> **❝** Those who know anything about the matter are aware that every writer, from Epicurus* to Bentham,* who maintained the theory of 'utility', meant by it, not something to be contradistinguished from pleasure, but pleasure itself, together with exemption from pain; and instead of opposing the useful to the agreeable or the ornamental, have always declared that 'useful' means these among other things. **❞**
>
> John Stuart Mill, *Utilitarianism*

pleasure. Mill responds to this misunderstanding by saying: "Those who know anything about the matter are aware that every writer, from Epicurus to Bentham, who maintained the theory of 'utility', meant by it, not something to be contradistinguished from pleasure, but pleasure itself, together with exemption from pain."[1]

Having made clear the meaning of utilitarianism, Mill tries to provide an empirical defense of it. He rejects other ethical positions such as ethical intuitionism,* and argues that morality is based on experience and observation. Mill is different from other utilitarians: he thinks that utilitarianism can be defended on *empirical* grounds (that is, through deduction based on observable evidence). The amendments he makes to the utilitarian doctrine itself also make him very different from earlier utilitarian thinkers.

Approach

In chapter 1 of *Utilitarianism*, Mill first dismisses alternative theories, especially those that depend on ethical intuitionism; in chapter 2, he defines utilitarianism and considers the objections to it listed above; in chapter 3 he considers possible motives for people to follow the principles of utilitarianism; in chapter 4 he offers his proof of utilitarianism; and in chapter 5 he focuses on justice and its relation to utility. Mill does not simply defend utilitarianism against its opponents, but also refines and develops the way it was presented by James Mill* (his father) and Jeremy Bentham. He ends up with his own version of utilitarianism.

The originality of *Utilitarianism* lies in its central claims and its empirical justification. The empirical justification aligns his work with the positivism* of the French social theorist August Comte;* according to positivist thought, scientific knowledge must be based on sensory experience and tested by experiment. Mill argues that the empirical proof for utilitarianism is that people all desire their own happiness:

"No reason can be given why the general happiness is desirable, except that each person, so far as he believes it to be attainable, desires his own happiness. This, however, being a fact, we have not only all the proof which the case admits of, but all which it is possible to require."[2]

So as well as creating his own version of utilitarianism and defending it against objections, Mill provides an empirical proof of the doctrine. This was original and unorthodox. It also contradicted those philosophers who believed that moral intuitions were the source of morality.

Contribution in Context

Mill's tutor Jeremy Bentham, in his *Principles of Morals and Legislation* (1789), claims that human beings are created to seek pleasure and to avoid pain, and that they desire pleasure for its own sake. He says there are physical, political, religious, and moral sources of sanctions for pleasure and pain. The political, religious, and moral sources, however, are secondary to the physical sources. The greatest happiness can only be achieved by maximizing pleasure and minimizing pain. An action or law is therefore good if it produces the greatest amount of pleasure and the least amount of pain to everyone involved. Bentham developed a scientific and rational method that could be used to measure quantities of pleasure and pain. He then applied it to the English legal system and institutions.

Although Mill does not abandon Bentham's fundamental principle (that of utility), he criticizes his predecessors, including his father, for offering an inadequate notion of the good (i.e. more overall happiness than unhappiness). As such, Mill revises utilitarianism and expands the notion of utility to include *qualitative* pleasure. This is a departure from the utilitarianism of his predecessors.

This departure has led to claims that Mill is an inconsistent utilitarian. His aims and intentions in *Utilitarianism* are, however, clearly presented and form a coherent, well-argued plan, even if there have been many interpretations of his arguments defending the principle of utility.* He is charged, for instance, with making a logical error in his central argument when he claims that from the thesis that "each person's happiness is a good to that person" it follows that the general happiness is "a good to the aggregate of all persons."[3] Critics of this argument have charged him with committing a fallacy of composition* (that is, an argument founded on the incorrect deduction that what is true for a part is true for the whole). Modern writers on Mill's *Utilitarianism*, such as the philosophy scholars Henry R. West,* David Lyons,* Jonathan Riley,* and John Skorupski,* have offered alternative interpretations of Mill's argument in an attempt to unearth what he actually intended.

NOTES

1   John Stuart Mill, *Utilitarianism*, ed. Roger Crisp (Oxford: Oxford University Press, 1998), 54.

2   Mill, *Utilitarianism,* 81.

3   Mill, *Utilitarianism*, 81.

SECTION 2
IDEAS

MODULE 5
MAIN IDEAS

KEY POINTS

- Mill argues that the foundation of morality is that an action is morally right if it promotes overall happiness, and morally wrong if it promotes the reverse.

- To assess whether an action promotes overall happiness, Mill says, we should not only look at the quantity of pleasure it will bring about—we should consider the quality of the pleasures that will be promoted, too.

- Although *Utilitarianism* is written clearly and accessibly, there is still debate about the precise meaning of certain passages.

Key Themes

The key themes of John Stuart Mill's *Utilitarianism* are the principles of utility, higher and lower pleasures, and the development of good moral character. The central thesis of the book is stated clearly as "the doctrine which accepts as the foundation of morals, Utility, or the Greatest Happiness Principle, holds that actions are right in proportion as they tend to promote happiness, wrong as they tend to produce the reverse of happiness."[1] In defending this claim, Mill endorses his tutor Jeremy Bentham's* greatest happiness principle* as the foundation of morality.[2]

The ultimate goal of human life is happiness. Everything that people desire is desired because it will either lead to happiness or provide some happiness. Happiness must therefore be the ultimate good. Mill defines happiness as "intended pleasure, and the absence of pain." He defines unhappiness as "pain, and the privation of

> **" The doctrine which accepts as the foundation of morals, Utility, or the Greatest Happiness Principle, holds that actions are right in proportion as they tend to promote happiness, wrong as they tend to produce the reverse of happiness. By happiness is intended pleasure, and the absence of pain; by unhappiness, pain, and the privation of pleasure. "**
>
> John Stuart Mill, *Utilitarianism*

pleasure."[3] Mill argues that it is not only one's actions that should be directed toward maximizing happiness: one's character should also aim to achieve this goal. Although Mill does not agree with Aristotle's* belief that it is one's character that makes an action right, he does nevertheless think that having a virtuous character is important, as it will make one likely to act in ways that will promote happiness in the world.

Mill then goes beyond Bentham by making a distinction between the *quantity* of pleasures that will be experienced in society and their *quality*. This is a response to critics of utilitarianism such as the Scottish thinker Thomas Carlyle,* who wrote that to "suppose that life has … no higher end than pleasure and no better and nobler object of desire and pursuit, they designate as utterly mean and groveling; as a doctrine worthy only of a swine."[4] Mill develops the crucially important idea that in addition to quantity, the *quality* of pleasures is important when measuring and ranking pleasures. Mill identifies two types of pleasure: higher pleasures (mental pleasures) such as poetry and knowledge; and lower pleasures (animalistic pleasures), such as sex and food. To find out which pleasure is qualitatively superior to another, one needs to check with those who have experienced both. Mill believes that individuals who have experienced higher pleasures prefer them to lower pleasures, and would not be willing to give them up even for "a promise of the fullest allowance of a beast's pleasures."[5] For Mill, higher pleasures are superior in quality and more desirable than lower pleasures.

Exploring the Ideas

Having defined happiness as the end (that is, the goal) of human life, Mill does not conclude that we should simply try to increase *our own* happiness. Instead, he thinks we ought to promote *overall* happiness—that is, the sum of happiness experienced throughout a society. This implies that in an imperfect world where not everyone is happy, we sometimes ought to sacrifice our own happiness for the happiness of others. Mill considers the "readiness to make such a sacrifice is the highest virtue which can be found in man."[6] But unlike other moral theories, Mill adds that self-sacrifice *as such* is not good or heroic: "a sacrifice which does not increase, or tend to increase, the sum total of happiness, it [utilitarianism] considers as wasted."[7] Utilitarianism says that morally right action must promote the *general* good, not just one's own. Mill therefore compares it to the Christian doctrine "to do as one would be done by, and to love one's neighbor as oneself." This, in Mill's view, "constitutes the ideal perfection of utilitarianism."[8]

The higher and lower pleasures that Mill distinguishes in his version of utilitarianism are based on the basic principle that "of two pleasures, if there be one to which all or almost all who have experience of both give a decided preference, irrespective of any feeling of moral obligation* to prefer it, that is the more desirable pleasure."[9] This may seem arbitrary, as it relies completely on what people prefer, but Mill thinks "no intelligent human being would consent to be a fool, no instructed person would be an ignoramus, no person of feeling and conscience would be selfish and base."[10] Mill therefore concludes, famously, that "it is better to be a human being satisfied than a pig satisfied; better to be Socrates satisfied than a fool satisfied."[11] Rather than being a "pig philosophy," Mill thinks that utilitarianism respects the *dignity* of human life and the pursuit of happiness of all individuals.

Language and Expression

Mill wrote *Utilitarianism* for the general reader; as the British political philosopher Alan Ryan* puts it, his audience were not trained logicians.[12] Mill lays out the common objections to utilitarianism in a clear style and responds to each in turn. The text is engaging, and the nature of the debate and the ideas are clear. He also defines concepts and offers reasons in support of utilitarianism.

Utilitarianism has, nevertheless, been difficult to interpret. Mill's contemporaries, including the philosophers George Edward Moore* and Francis H. Bradley,* dismissed the text as inconsistent. Modern scholars such as Henry R. West* and David Lyons,* however, have offered a different picture. Mill's ideas are useful to students and academics in the fields of ethics and politics as he deals with concepts that remain relevant today, such as utilitarianism, security, justice, and liberty. Academic debates on the nature of morality and liberalism have frequently made reference to Mill's ideas, and many academic books have been devoted to analyzing his thought. Many people, including politicians and policy makers, take decisions based on utilitarian considerations, although it is difficult to tell whether they draw on Mill's specific ideas or on utilitarian thought in general.

NOTES

1   John Stuart Mill, *Utilitarianism*, ed. Roger Crisp (Oxford: Oxford University Press, 1998), chapter 2.

2   Mill, *Utilitarianism*, 55.

3   Mill, *Utilitarianism*, 55.

4   Mill, *Utilitarianism*, 55.

5   Mill, *Utilitarianism*, 57.

6   Mill, *Utilitarianism*, 63.

7   Mill, *Utilitarianism*, 63–4.

8   Mill, *Utilitarianism*, 64.

9   Mill, *Utilitarianism*, 56.

10 Mill, *Utilitarianism*, 56–7.

11 Mill, Utilitarianism, 57.

12 Alan Ryan, *John Stuart Mill* (London: Routledge & Kegan Paul, 1974).

MODULE 6
SECONDARY IDEAS

KEY POINTS

- Mill argues that we are motivated to act according to utilitarian principles because of our conscience and our sympathy with others.

- Mill claims that justice and utilitarianism as a moral philosophy are entirely compatible and that security is of great importance for utilitarianism.

- Although the chapter on the relationship between justice and utility is the longest in the book, it has received relatively little attention in the literature.

Other Ideas

Having identified happiness as the goal of human life and defined the principle of utility* in *Utilitarianism*, John Stuart Mill went on to address a series of further concerns. Three themes in particular are worth singling out: motivation, justice, and security.

The first of these is our *motivation* to act in the morally right way. This is an important issue, because it addresses a tension in the utilitarian position; on the one hand, Mill says that our own happiness is the end (that is, the goal) of our life; it is what we all pursue. On the other hand, he claims that morally good actions often involve a sacrifice of one's own happiness for the sake of the general good. If the first claim is true, how could we be motivated to act on the basis of the second claim? Mill's answer is that our *conscience* and our *sympathy* toward mankind motivate us to do so. Or, as he puts it, we are motivated by "the social feelings of mankind; the desire to be in unity with our fellow creatures."[1]

> **❝** The ultimate sanction, therefore, of all morality
> (external motives apart) being a subjective feeling
> in our own minds, I see nothing embarrassing to
> those whose standard is utility, in the question, what
> is the sanction of that particular standard? We may
> answer, the same as of all other moral standards: the
> conscientious feelings of mankind. **❞**
>
> John Stuart Mill, *Utilitarianism*

The second theme is the concern that utilitarianism might conflict with justice. Utilitarianism is about maximizing the happiness of the greatest number of people. But critics argue that to achieve this, the interests of some people might sometimes have to be sacrificed for the sake of others. This would be unjust. For instance, an innocent person might have to be imprisoned in order to stop an angry crowd rioting; the imprisonment would lead to a greater overall happiness (it prevents a riot), but it would be an injustice for the innocent prisoner. Mill devotes his final chapter to proving that justice is vital for utilitarianism and does not conflict at all with the utilitarian view.

A third idea that Mill develops in *Utilitarianism* is that of security. Although *Utilitarianism* focuses mainly on happiness, Mill recognizes that a sense of security is crucial for people to feel happy. He introduces a political and legal element to the text, arguing that we should promote conditions that give people a sense of security in their lives.

Exploring the Ideas

Mill argues that our conscience and our sympathy toward others motivate us to act morally; he does not believe that morality comes from external sanctions, such as laws, social punishment, or godly disapproval. The ultimate sanction of all morality, Mill claims, is "a subjective feeling in our own minds"—namely, "the conscientious feelings of mankind."[2] This is clever reasoning on Mill's behalf, as he can now claim that by helping others, we in fact serve our own happiness. He writes that "so long as [people] are co-operating, their ends are identified with those of others; there is at least a temporary feeling that the interests of others are their own interests."[3] When we sacrifice ourselves for the general happiness of others, we satisfy the desires of our conscience. This gives us intense pleasure and explains why we are motivated to act in such a way.

Mill argues that utilitarianism is not opposed to justice; rather, the idea of justice can be explained in terms of utility. He concludes that feelings about justice are based on the belief that people's behavior, social institutions, and social policies should not undermine our own happiness or the happiness of anyone else. In Mill's words: "The sentiment of justice appears to me to be, the animal desire to repel or retaliate a hurt or damage to oneself, or to those with whom one sympathizes, widened so as to include all persons, by the human capacity of enlarged sympathy, and the human conception of intelligent self-interest."[4] Mill thinks what is just is not opposed to the principles of utilitarianism. The two are compatible and justice is *required* and *grounded* by utilitarianism.

This gives us a direct grip on our third theme—why Mill thinks security is so important. Mill regards security as something that no person can do without, and calls it "the most vital of all interests."[5] Although people want a wide range of things, they all have an interest in furthering security. Since security is a common interest, in that everyone shares it, it should be maximized for all. It is therefore in the interest of all of us to promote security since in the long run our own individual interests will also be looked after. When our security is in danger, we think in terms of injustices, though in the end the importance of moral security is explained by utility—the ultimate good.

Overlooked

John Stuart Mill's *Utilitarianism* is a short work that has been subjected to serious scrutiny. One would think that no part of it has been neglected. Most analysis, however, has focused on particular passages of chapters 2 and 4, rather than providing an interpretation of the entire book. The final chapter that examines the relation between justice and utilitarianism has received far less attention than chapter 4, which attempts to prove that the principle of utility is true.

This could be due to the fact that early responses to *Utilitarianism* concentrated on Mill's proof of the principle of utility. Such thinkers, including the British philosophers Francis H. Bradley* and George Edward Moore,* tried to prove that Mill had committed a number of logical fallacies.* Modern scholars such as Henry R. West,* David Lyons,* Jonathan Riley,* and John Skorupski* have continued to draw on these earlier objections to Mill's proof of the principle of utility. As a result, the chapter on proofs has been the most popular among scholars.

NOTES

1   John Stuart Mill, *Utilitarianism*, ed. Roger Crisp (Oxford: Oxford University Press, 1998), 77.

2   Mill, *Utilitarianism*, 75.

3   Mill, *Utilitarianism*, 78.

4   Mill, *Utilitarianism,* 97.

5   Mill, *Utilitarianism*, 98.

MODULE 7
ACHIEVEMENT

KEY POINTS

- *Utilitarianism* develops the utilitarian views of the social reformer and philosopher Jeremy Bentham,* clarifies what utilitarianism is, and defends it against common criticisms.

- The text developed utilitarianism into one of the most important positions in moral philosophy and is ranked among the greatest works in moral philosophy.

- The text appears to contain logical fallacies,* however: it fails to clarify how higher and lower pleasures can affect calculations of overall happiness, and it is not clear whether Mill supported "rule utilitarianism"* or "act utilitarianism"* (two different ways of understanding what might define a "right" action).

Assessing the Argument

John Stuart Mill's main aim in *Utilitarianism* is to clarify utilitarianism as a position in moral philosophy, to develop the utilitarian views of the thinker Jeremy Bentham, and to defend his own version of utilitarianism against its critics. In this respect, the book has been a great success. Mill stated more clearly than anyone before him what utilitarianism is, and his distinction between higher and lower pleasures has had a lasting influence on debates in moral philosophy. His responses to critics of utilitarianism are detailed and full of insight. His proof of utilitarianism offered in chapter 4, although disputed, continues to attract attention. It has helped make utilitarianism the most widely supported view in moral philosophy today.

> **"** *Utilitarianism* is one of the most significant works in moral philosophy, ranking in importance alongside Aristotle's* Nicomachean Ethics and Immanuel Kant's* Groundwork of the Metaphysic of Morals. **"**
>
> Roger Crisp, *Routledge Philosophy Guidebook to Mill on Utilitarianism*

Utilitarianism is both one of the most important books in moral philosophy and the most widely read statement of utilitarian ideas. It is widely used in colleges and universities to introduce students to moral philosophy or ethics. The text's core arguments have been subject to numerous interpretations, even if no consensus has yet been reached on some issues. Scholars continue to debate the proper interpretation of Mill's arguments and his philosophical position.

Achievement in Context

When Mill wrote his text, utilitarianism was in decline as a respectable view in moral philosophy. In fact, Bentham's utilitarianism had faced serious criticisms and was viewed with suspicion by the majority of intellectuals of his time. Mill's text played a key role in strengthening the utilitarian position, to the point that it became a major force not only in philosophy but also in everyday politics.

Mill attacked ethical intuitionism*—the notion, very roughly, that it was possible to arrive at an understanding of ethical behavior through intuition alone—and said that the principle of utility,* not the will of God, was the foundation of morals. He also modified Bentham's version of utilitarianism. It is therefore not surprising that he was criticized by a wide range of thinkers, particularly intuitionists, fellow utilitarians, and religious scholars.

Despite these criticisms, his work was considered the best statement of utilitarianism available.[1] When the Irish historian and political theorist William E. H. Lecky* controversially failed to mention Mill in his *History of European Morals* (1869), even opponents of utilitarianism criticized him. They felt that Mill's utilitarianism was the best version of the doctrine and, as such, deserved attention.[2] According to the American scholar Jerome B. Schneewind,* the controversy marked the "point at which it became generally clear that to deal with utilitarianism one had to deal with Mill's version of it."[3]

Limitations

One limitation of Mill's *Utilitarianism* is that it seems to rely on a number of fallacies.* To go from his claim that happiness is the greatest good to the idea that we should therefore promote the *general* good has been viewed as a false inference. The fallacy he has been accused of is the "fallacy of composition,"* which arises when one infers that what is true of a part or parts is true of the whole ("all the parts of a bicycle are light; therefore a bicycle is light," for example). So although it may be true that *personal* happiness is our own ultimate good, it does not follow that *general* happiness is the ultimate good when we take all people together.

A second limitation is that Mill did not say how the difference between higher and lower pleasures should be calculated, other than stating that higher pleasures should have greater weight. According to Bentham's version of utilitarianism, every pleasure has equal value, and each individual unit of pleasure (sometimes called "utils") can be counted and added together. Precisely how that is meant to work in Mill's view of utilitarianism remains unclear.

A third limitation is that Mill defends a combination of what are now known as "rule utilitarianism" and "act utilitarianism." According to act utilitarianism, the moral goodness of an action depends on the degree to which *that action* affects the total amount of happiness. According to rule utilitarianism, by contrast, the moral goodness of an action depends on whether it fits with *rules* that generally positively affect the total amount of happiness. This is an importance difference, as it can lead to contradictory claims about whether an action is right or not. Killing, for instance, can sometimes greatly increase the totality of happiness, although killing in general will not. Mill is not clear about which version of utilitarianism he supports. In defining utilitarianism early in the text, he writes that "*actions* are right in proportion as they tend to promote happiness, wrong as they tend to produce the reverse of happiness."[4] But a few pages later he writes that "the end [that is, the goal] of human action, is necessarily also the standard of morality; which may accordingly be defined, *the rules and precepts for human conduct*, by the observance of which an existence such as has been described might be, to the greatest extent possible, secured to all mankind."[5] In recent years, the British scholar of ethics Roger Crisp* has favored an interpretation of Mill along the lines of act utilitarianism.[6] Others have preferred the elements highlighted by rule utilitarianism.[7] And some think that we can find both elements in Mill's text.[8]

NOTES

1 J. B. Schneewind, "Concerning Some Criticisms of Mill's *Utilitarianism, 1861–76,*" in *James and John Stuart Mill: Papers of the Centenary Conference*, eds. John M. Robson and Michael Laine (Toronto and Buffalo: University of Toronto Press, 1976).

2 Schneewind, "Concerning Some Criticisms," 40.

3 Schneewind, "Concerning Some Criticisms," 40.

4 John Stuart Mill, *Utilitarianism*, ed. Roger Crisp (Oxford: Oxford University Press, 1998), 55.

5 Mill, *Utilitarianism*, 59.

6 See Roger Crisp, *Routledge Philosophy Guidebook to Mill on Utilitarianism* (London: Routledge, 1977), 102.

7 See Dale E. Miller, *John Stuart Mill: Moral, Social and Political Thought* (Cambridge: Cambridge University Press, 2010).

8 See Henry R. West, *An Introduction to Mill's Ethics* (Cambridge: Cambridge University Press, 2004).

MODULE 8
PLACE IN THE AUTHOR'S WORK

KEY POINTS

- Mill's moral philosophy is presented most clearly and systematically in *Utilitarianism*. But many of these ideas were prepared in earlier essays and publications by Mill.

- Mill's work shows great consistency of thinking over his lifetime, revealing a clear commitment to individual liberty and the increase of happiness for all.

- *Utilitarianism* is the most important of all his works and is as relevant today as it was when it was first published.

Positioning

John Stuart Mill started writing at an early age, contributing sophisticated articles in newspapers and periodicals before he was twenty. By the time *Utilitarianism* was published in 1861, he had already produced a number of essays and books and was regarded as one of the leading philosophers in Britain. His first major published text was *A System of Logic, Ratiocinative and Inductive* (1843), which argued in favor of logic as a method of proof and also targeted intuitionists.* In 1848, Mill published *Principles of Political Economy*, which became a major text in economic theory.

Mill's essay "On Liberty" (1859) offers a defense of individual liberty and argues that conduct that causes harm to others should be restricted. He returns to this theme in chapter 5 of *Utilitarianism*. Mill says it is entirely appropriate for society to interfere with individual behavior to prevent harm to others. In *Considerations on Representative Government* (1861) he argues for a form of government in Britain that is both representative and has greater public involvement. He says

> **❝** [Many] of the issues discussed in *Utilitarianism* were foreshadowed in earlier essays by Mill: the foundation of ethics and ethical understanding, the importance of first and secondary principles, the proof of utilitarianism, the sources of human happiness, moral motivation and the 'sanctions' of morality. **❞**
>
> Roger Crisp, *Routledge Philosophy Guidebook to Mill on Utilitarianism*

that public voting "ensures that opinion will be mobilized to both preserve and induce the public good."[1] In *Subjection of Women* (1869), he argues for the emancipation* of women and equality between the sexes. These texts show Mill's vision of a liberal society consisting of two parts: "creative individuality and the unity of will needed to sustain society."[2] They also reveal the development of a liberal doctrine grounded in utilitarianism. As the scholar Roger Crisp* concludes in his overview of Mill's work, "many of the issues discussed in *Utilitarianism* were foreshadowed in earlier essays by Mill."[3]

Integration

Despite the fact that Mill wrote on a range of different topics, his work demonstrates remarkable unity and consistency. In his *System of Logic*, written nearly 20 years before *Utilitarianism*, Mill attacked intuitionists. He argued that if one is an intuitionist about ethics, then one should logically also be an intuitionist about science and accept that we can discover laws of nature without the help of observation. He considered this to be an absurd position. His attack on intuitionism in *Utilitarianism* was clearly foreshadowed in his earlier work, as part of a long-term effort to promote empiricism* in all areas of human knowledge.

In *On Liberty* (1959) Mill offers a defense of individual liberty:

people, he argues, should be allowed to act as they see fit, the only exception being if they intend to harm others. The latter qualification is the so-called harm principle, which states that "the only purpose for which power can be rightfully exercised over any member of a civilized community, against his will, is to prevent harm to others."[4] These are two themes that surface again in *Utilitarianism*, where Mill argues, first, that moral rightness consists in maximizing pleasure and minimizing pain and suffering. This means that people should not be impeded unless they do indeed harm others and so reduce the total sum of happiness. Second, Mill commits to the view that every person is of equal worth and that the happiness of each individual matters. One group cannot use others as a mere instrument to their own benefit. Maximizing the aggregate of happiness implies that each person has an equal claim to happiness.

Finally, in his *Subjection of Women* (1869), Mill extends his arguments to imply that women should have equal rights with men. Again, the maximization of the sum of all happiness is the main goal that inspires Mill. In his view this should include women as much as men; hence his passionate plea for the emancipation of women in nineteenth-century Britain.

Significance

The two best-known works of John Stuart Mill are *On Liberty* and *Utilitarianism*. *Utilitarianism* offers the most systematic and precise presentation of Mill's moral philosophy, drawing together a number of themes that had been in preparation since his early youth. Roger Crisp suggests that "in so far as Mill was an evangelist, *Utilitarianism*, first published as a series of three essays in 1861, can be seen as his bible."[5]

Mill was already well known as one of the most significant philosophers in Britain during his lifetime. *Utilitarianism* was not written for a small intellectual elite, however. It was published as a series of three essays in 1861 in *Fraser's Magazine for Town and Country*, a general and literary periodical that was founded in London in 1830 and aimed at a middle-class readership. Its first publication as a book was in 1863, and it was only then that Mill added the chapter on utility and justice.

Mill's reputation has changed little over the last 150 years. He is still considered a giant in philosophy. Most university courses in politics, economics, and moral philosophy deal extensively with Mill's views, especially those expressed in *Utilitarianism*. These views have lost none of their force or urgency, and it is unlikely that their significance will lessen any time soon.

NOTES

1   Robert Devigne, *Reforming Liberalism: J. S. Mill's use of Ancient, Religious, Liberal, and Romantic Moralities* (New Haven, CT: Yale University Press, 2006), 218.

2   Devigne, *Routledge Philosophy Reforming Liberalism*, 219.

3   See Roger Crisp, *Routledge Philosophy Guidebook to Mill on Utilitarianism*. (London: Routledge, 1977), 12.

4   John Stuart Mill, *On Liberty* (London: Penguin, 2010), 21.

5   Crisp, *Routledge Philosophy Guidebook to Mill*, 7.

SECTION 3
IMPACT

MODULE 9
THE FIRST RESPONSES

KEY POINTS

- Most of the early responses to Mill's *Utilitarianism* were hostile. He was criticized for making fallacious—that is, badly reasoned—inferences and being disloyal to the utilitarian position.

- Mill did not revise his arguments in light of these criticisms. Instead he tried to clarify what it was he had actually argued.

- There was no consensus on Mill's disputed claims during his lifetime. Indeed, debates on the true interpretation of Mill's views continue to this day.

Criticism

The majority of responses to John Stuart Mill's *Utilitarianism* in the first 15 years after its publication were hostile. Critics focused on alleged logical flaws in his arguments.[1] Four issues in particular were raised—namely, "his views on the derivability of moral notions from non-moral ones; his … 'proof' of the principle of utility;* his distinction between higher and lower pleasures; and his claim that the rules of common-sense morality may be taken as the middle axioms [that is, accepted truths] of a utilitarian ethic."[2] Early critics such as George Edward Moore* questioned whether Mill's proof of the principle of utility was a fallacy.*[3] Mill tried to prove the principle of utility with the following argument:

"The only proof capable of being given that an object is visible, is that people actually see it. The only proof that sound is audible, is that people hear it … In like manner, I apprehend the sole evidence it is possible to

> **❝** [When] I said that the general happiness is a good to the aggregate of all persons I did not mean that every human being's happiness is a good to every other human being; though I think in a good state of society and education it would be so. **❞**
>
> John Stuart Mill, *The Letters of John Stuart Mill*

produce that anything is desirable, is that people do actually desire it."[4]

Moore accused Mill of drawing a false analogy between "desirable" and "visible," objecting that "the fallacy in this step is so obvious, that it is quite wonderful how he failed to see it. The fact is that 'desirable' does not mean 'able to be desired' as 'visible' means 'able to be seen'. The desirable simply means what *ought* to be desired or *deserves* to be desired."[5]

The influential philosopher Thomas H. Green,* in turn, objects to the claim that pleasure is the only object of desire. He points out that the object of desire and the pleasure produced from satisfying that desire are not the same.[6] For example, when we are hungry we do not seek pleasure, but food; so in this case, pleasure should not be seen as the object of desire. Moore, Green, and the philosopher Francis H. Bradley* were among early critics of Mill's distinction between quantitative and qualitative pleasures (that is, pleasures measured by quantity and those measured by quality) and questioned his use of the doctrine of hedonism.*[7]

It is important to note that not everyone objected to Mill's defense of utilitarianism. The Scottish philosopher James Seth,* for example, vigorously defended Mill's position in an article published in 1908.[8]

Responses

Utilitarianism had been through four editions by 1871, with relatively minor revisions and additions. The philosopher Alexander Bain,* in his 1882 work entitled *John Stuart Mill*, said that he was "not aware that any change was made in reprinting [the first edition of *Utilitarianism*] as a volume, notwithstanding that it had its full share of hostile criticism as it came out in *Fraser*."[9] This implies that Mill did not respond to initial criticisms of his work in later editions. The American scholar Jerome Schneewind,* however, takes issue with the level of attention the work initially received. He claims that for the first seven or eight years *Utilitarianism* did not receive much attention in print, even though philosophical responses to the text were largely negative.[10]

Mill's argument that "happiness is a good: that each person's happiness is a good to that person, and the general happiness, therefore, a good to the aggregate of all persons"[11] has been the cause of much debate and has led to the charge of being a fallacy of composition.* Mill was aware of this criticism, and in a letter to a correspondent dated June 13, 1868, he makes his position clear: "I merely meant … to argue that since A's happiness is a good, B's a good, C's a good, etc., the sum of these must be a good."[12]

Mill wrote the letter before the publication of Francis Bradley's critical essay published in his *Ethical Studies*. But Bradley failed to respond to it, instead rejecting the proof as Mill had stated it in *Utilitarianism*. It should be pointed out, though, that in Mill's letter he still proposes a general principle that if one puts good things together, one will end up with a good whole; Bradley's critique therefore still seems fair.[13]

Conflict and Consensus

Mill died in 1873, and after his death his opponents unleashed a wholesale attack on his version of utilitarianism. In the years that followed, a huge range of texts was produced both supporting and opposing those objections. The letters Mill wrote toward the end of his life suggest that he had not changed his views, believing that most of his critics had simply failed to understand him. Critics such as Bradley, in turn, paid no attention to the clarifications that Mill had added to his text. Instead they continued to point out what they thought was wrong in Mill's published version of *Utilitarianism*.

The debate over the correct interpretation of Mill's core ideas continues today. It is largely a repeat of earlier responses to Mill's core arguments. However, a number of modern scholars, among them Henry R. West* and David Lyons,* have provided a revisionist interpretation of Mill's utilitarianism—that is, an interpretation that questions orthodox opinion—arguing that his critics misread him. But there is a risk that in defending Mill against past and present critics, an inaccurate view is attributed to him. The conflict over Mill's defense of utilitarianism is nevertheless bound to continue for some time.

NOTES

1 J. B. Schneewind, "Concerning Some Criticisms of Mill's *Utilitarianism*, 1861–76," in *James and John Stuart Mill: Papers of the Centenary Conference*, eds. John M. Robson and Michael Laine (Toronto and Buffalo: University of Toronto Press, 1976).

2 Schneewind, "Concerning Some Criticisms," 41.

3 George Edward Moore, *Principia Ethica* (Cambridge: Cambridge University Press, 1903).

4 John Stuart Mill, *Utilitarianism*, ed. Roger Crisp (Oxford: Oxford University Press, 1998), 81.

5 Moore, *Principia Ethica*, 67.

6 Thomas Hill Green, *Prolegomena to Ethics* (Oxford: Clarendon Press, 2003).

7 See Moore, *Principia Ethica*; Green, *Prolegomena to Ethics*; Francis Herbert Bradley, *Ethical Studies* (London: Oxford University Press, 1962).

8 James Seth, "The Alleged Fallacies in Mill's 'Utilitarianism'," *The Philosophical Review* 17, no. 5 (1908): 469–88.

9 Cited in Schneewind, "Concerning Some Criticisms," 38.

10 Schneewind, "Concerning Some Criticisms."

11 Mill, *Utilitarianism*, 81.

12 John Stuart Mill, *The Letters of John Stuart Mill,* vol. 2, ed. with an introduction by Hugh S. R. Elliot, and a note on Mill's private life by Mary Taylor (New York: Longmans, Green & Co), 116.

13 Bradley, *Ethical Studies*, 113, n.1.

MODULE 10
THE EVOLVING DEBATE

KEY POINTS

- In the second half of the twentieth century utilitarianism became a major force in moral philosophy. It was further developed—but heavily criticized, too.

- In recent decades, many new schools of utilitarianism have been formed, including "two-level utilitarianism,"* "rule utilitarianism,"* and "preference utilitarianism."*

- Scholarship on utilitarianism is now common in a variety of academic disciplines, in both theoretical and applied form.

Uses and Problems

At the time of John Stuart Mill's death in 1873, empiricism,* which had dominated British philosophical thought and shaped *Utilitarianism*, had lost its position, first to idealism* (the philosophical position, very roughly, that "reality" is primarily a question of perception), and later to logical positivism* (the philosophical position that to be cognitively meaningful, a statement must be empirically verified or logically inferred from empirically verifiable statements). Little attention was paid to Mill's social philosophy until the second half of the twentieth century, when scholars such as Carl Wellman,* who specializes in ethics and philosophy of law, began to offer responses to the traditional criticisms of Mill's "proof" of the principle of utility.* Since then, commentators such as Henry R. West,* David Lyons,* and Jonathan Riley*[1] have offered a revisionist interpretation of Mill's work, including explanations of how the principle of utility can be proven.

> **❝** It is absurd to demand of ... a man, when the sums come in from the utility network which the projects of others have in part determined, that he should just step aside from his own project and decision and acknowledge the decision which utilitarian calculation requires. **❞**
>
> J. J. C. Smart and Bernard Williams, *Utilitarianism: For and Against*

In the latter half of the twentieth century utilitarianism again became a major force in moral philosophy, with Mill's work being of central interest. Philosophers have expanded his version of utilitarianism in recent decades, forming new versions, finding new arguments in support of it, and introducing refinements.

At the same time, new criticisms of utilitarianism have also appeared. Three of these have become especially popular in the literature. The first is the idea of the "pleasure machine," introduced by the influential political philosopher Robert Nozick.* Nozick argues that if we were given the possibility to be hooked up to a machine that kept us permanently in a state of pleasure, most people would not describe this as a good life, despite the quantity of pleasure.[2] The second is the British thinker Philippa Foot's* famous trolley problem: pulling a lever so that an oncoming train kills one person instead of five seems morally different from pushing one person in front of the train to save five people's lives. Although the consequences are identical (one dead, five saved), the thought experiment tries to show that it is not just the results of our actions that matter in moral evaluations (as Mill says), but also our intentions.[3] And third, the British moral philosopher Bernard Williams* has also offered thought experiments intended to show that it can in fact be extremely immoral to act upon the greatest happiness principle. All these experiments question whether the principle of utility can be the foundation of all morality.[4]

Schools of Thought

Since the 1960s a number of different schools in utilitarianism have evolved. Here we shall focus on three such schools: rule utilitarianism,* two-level utilitarianism,* and preference utilitarianism.*

In 1953 the British philosopher James Opie Urmson* published an article arguing that Mill justifies moral rules ("Do not steal" and "Do not kill," for example) on the basis of the principle of utility.[5] The school of "rule utilitarianism"*—founded on the view that the moral goodness of an act depends on whether it obeys *rules* that generally increase the total amount of happiness—emerged after this. This view was developed to make it easier to calculate how much happiness or unhappiness an action might bring about. It is a view that, in its turn, has also received a great deal of criticism.

To overcome the limitations of rule utilitarianism, the British philosopher R. M. Hare* developed a view called "two-level utilitarianism." According to this school, although we should follow rules based on the principle of utility, in exceptional circumstances we may perform actions that break those rules. In these exceptional cases we are to take the position of act utilitarianism,* and assess (regardless of general rules) whether an action promotes happiness or not.[6] Two-level utilitarianism therefore combines rule and act utilitarianism.

The third important school is "preference utilitarianism," first developed by the Nobel prize-winning economist John Harsanyi,* but mainly associated with the Australian moral philosopher Peter Singer.*[7] This school argues that we are not in fact motivated to maximize pleasure and to minimize pain, but instead we are driven mainly to satisfy our own preferences. Like Mill, preference utilitarians claim that good actions promote good consequences. But unlike Mill, they believe that consequences will be good when they allow people to satisfy their own preferences.

In Current Scholarship

The importance of utilitarianism in current scholarship is hard to overstate. Utilitarianism is a major force in philosophy, psychology, economy, and politics. Virtually everyone dealing with normative* questions (questions concerning what is considered to be the normal or correct way of doing something), whether practical or theoretical, has to take a position on whether utilitarianism offers a suitable guide to what the right course of action is. Some scholars have focused on understanding precisely what thinkers like Jeremy Bentham* and Mill meant in their definitions, assertions, and arguments. Others point out what is wrong either with utilitarianism in general, or with specific versions of it. Still others are developing the utilitarian vision further and, like Mill, continue to defend it against its critics.

Utilitarianism plays a major role in applied ethics. For instance, debates about animal welfare have been approached from a utilitarian point of view. Animals can experience pleasure and pain, so there is clearly an argument that overall happiness or unhappiness should include that of animals. There are also debates in bioethics, where utilitarianism can help decide, for instance, which patients in health care should get public money. Areas such as poverty have also been approached from a utilitarian perspective. Utilitarianism is therefore developed—and also criticized—not just on a theoretical level, but also in a wide variety of applied forms.

NOTES

1   See Jonathan Riley, "Mill's Extraordinary Moral Theory," *Politics, Philosophy and Economics* 9, no. 1 (2010): 67–116.

2   See Robert Nozick, *Anarchy, State, and Utopia* (New York: Basic Books, 1974), 42–5.

3   See Philippa Foot, "The Problem of Abortion and the Doctrine of the Double Effect," in *Virtues and Vices* (Oxford: Basil Blackwell, 1978).

4   See J. J. C. Smart and Bernard Williams, *Utilitarianism: For and Against* (Cambridge: Cambridge University Press, 1973).

5   J. O. Urmson, "The Interpretation of the Moral Philosophy of J.S. Mill," *The Philosophical Quarterly* 3 (1953): 33–9.

6   See R. M. Hare, *Proceedings of the Aristotelian Society, New Series* 73 (1972–73): 1–18.

7   See John Harsanyi, "Morality and the Theory of Rational Behaviour," in *Utilitarianism and Beyond*, eds. Amartya Sen and Bernard Williams (Cambridge: Cambridge University Press, 1982), 39–62; Peter Singer, *Practical Ethics* (Cambridge: Cambridge University Press, 1979).

MODULE 11
IMPACT AND INFLUENCE TODAY

KEY POINTS

- *Utilitarianism* is viewed as a classic work in the history of philosophy. But it still inspires contemporary utilitarians who support their views with the insights offered by Mill.

- *Utilitarianism* is one of the three major traditions in moral philosophy—and Mill has powerful arguments why the other two might be reducible to utilitarianism.

- Philosophical debates about utilitarianism continue, with those over the "consequentializing" move becoming increasingly important.

Position

John Stuart Mill's *Utilitarianism* is both one of the most important books in moral philosophy and the most widely read account of utilitarianism. It has been widely used in colleges and universities to introduce students to moral philosophy or ethics. It is a classic text in the history of philosophy. Contemporary philosophers still refer to it, either to support their own strand of utilitarianism, or to criticize or defend aspects of utilitarianism that were already present in Mill's ideas. Modern utilitarians such as the Australian moral philosopher Peter Singer,* for instance, who believe they are continuing Mill's project of defending utilitarianism, continue to reference the text.

In debates about the nature of justice, *Utilitarianism* also continues to be an important source, mainly because of the fifth chapter, in which Mill lays out his view on the relationship between utility and justice. John Rawls,* the famous twentieth-century theoretician of justice, directly refers to *Utilitarianism* when criticizing the view that

> **❝** Current trends in philosophy make it easier to appreciate Mill, to rethink his work and put it to use, than it has been for a hundred years or more. **❞**
>
> John Skorupski, "Introduction," in *Cambridge Companion to Mill*

utility maximization is the foundation of justice.[1] Rawls considers it unjust to sacrifice the interests of a single individual in order to benefit others (according to utilitarianism, the morally right thing to do in some situations) unless the individual whose interests are sacrificed is compensated in some way. In developing this argument, Rawls engages directly with Mill's *Utilitarianism*. Mill's text is by no means an antiquated classic in the history of ideas. Despite the developments in the utilitarian tradition, it continues to hold a central place in contemporary moral philosophy.

Interaction

Utilitarianism is generally seen as one of the three major traditions in moral philosophy; Kantian deontology* (a moral philosophy centered on notions of duty) and Aristotelian virtue ethics* (a moral philosophy centered on the cultivation of virtuous behavior) are the two others. In *Utilitarianism*, Mill presents arguments against both traditions. He holds that when Kant says we should never act on a principle that cannot be universalized, "all he shows is that the *consequences* of their universal adoption would be such as no one would choose to incur."[2] Mill is more favorable toward virtue ethicists, especially with respect to their emphasis on education and development of good character. But again, he thinks that the reason *why* a good character is so important is best explained by the utility principle: good character will result in the performance of better activities. It will also lead to a greater amount of overall happiness, which is our main goal in life.

In his criticism of these traditions, Mill in fact turns virtue ethics and Kantian deontology into forms of utilitarianism. This type of attack on Kantian deontology and virtue ethics has been revived in recent years and labeled "consequentializing."[3] "To consequentialize," as one contributor to the debates writes, "is to take a putatively non-consequentialist moral theory and show that it is actually just another form of consequentialism."[4] Consequentializers agree with Mill that what ultimately matters is bringing about good consequences. Despite the difficulties that utilitarianism faces, in recent years this has proven to be a major challenge to schools in moral philosophy that focus on things other than consequences (intentions, for example, or character traits).

The Continuing Debate

The contemporary debates on utilitarianism take many forms. First, contemporary philosophers continue to identify which position classical utilitarians such as Jeremy Bentham* and John Stuart Mill actually defended. In addition to the contributions of Henry R. West,* David Lyons,* Jonathan Riley,* and John Skorupski,* it is worth referring to a recent book by Fred Rosen of University College London titled *Classical Utilitarianism from Hume to Mill* (2003).[5] Second, philosophers continue to debate the validity of utilitarianism. The criticisms offered by Robert Nozick,* Philippa Foot,* and Bernard Williams* have sparked a great many responses from philosophers working today.

And third, the specific attack that consequentializers make on Kantian deontology and virtue ethics is debated among moral philosophers. Many Kantians and virtue ethicists have tried to come up with responses as to why their specific view cannot be "consequentialized." The professor of moral philosophy Christine Korsgaard* argues in a recent paper that neither Kant's nor Aristotle's position can be consequentialized, because the idea of a *general* good, one that is not good *for* someone, is incoherent.[6]

Although these debates are very recent and it will no doubt take some time before consensus is reached, it is worth pointing out that the "consequentializing move" has its roots in Mill's text. For these, as well as many other reasons, Skorupski, a professor of moral philosophy, claims that "current trends in philosophy make it easier to appreciate Mill, to rethink his work and put it to use, than it has been for a hundred years or more."[7]

NOTES

1   John Rawls, *A Theory of Justice* (Cambridge, MA: Belknap Press of Harvard University, 1971).

2   John Stuart Mill, *Utilitarianism*, ed. Roger Crisp (Oxford: Oxford University Press, 1998), 52.

3   Campbell Brown, "Consequentialise This," *Ethics* 121, no. 4 (2011): 749–71.

4   Brown, "Consequentialise This," 749.

5   Fred Rosen, *Classical Utilitarianism from Hume to Mill* (London: Routledge, 2003).

6   Christine Korsgaard, "On Having a Good," *Philosophy: The Journal of the Royal Institute of Philosophy* 89, no. 3 (2014): 405–29.

7   John Skorpuski, "Introduction," in *Cambridge Companion to Mill*, ed. John Skorupski (Cambridge, Cambridge University Press, 1998), 2.

MODULE 12
WHERE NEXT?

KEY POINTS

- *Utilitarianism* will continue to be important, not only as an introductory text to utilitarianism, but also as a rich source for further developments of the theory.

- Contemporary philosophers continue to build on Mill's central arguments, trying to defend him against the criticisms that have been leveled against these arguments.

- *Utilitarianism* is a key text in moral philosophy because it is the first thorough and systematic explanation and defense of utilitarianism, supported by evidence.

Potential

We must assume that John Stuart Mill's *Utilitarianism* will continue to have an important influence in moral philosophy, economics, and political theory. As a clear and systematic presentation of utilitarianism, it will continue to serve as the founding text of one of the most important and popular theories in moral philosophy. The utilitarian tradition has grown extensively over the last decades. Several different schools of utilitarianism now argue over how to define the utility principle, in terms of acts, rules, or preferences, and so on. Although in recent years the hedonistic* (that is, pleasure-oriented) aspects of Mill's views have given way to the preference utilitarianism advanced by the notable Australian moral philosopher Peter Singer* and others, the text continues to have great appeal to modern moral philosophers.

Less attention has been paid to Mill in recent years in the

> **❝** Since it is short, readable, polemical and eloquent, it has always offered an easy way into the complexities of moral philosophy and into the creed of the utilitarian movement. **❞**
>
> Alan Ryan, "Introduction," *Utilitarianism and Other Essays*

literature on political liberalism. Liberal thinkers have focused instead on the highly influential twentieth-century moral philosopher John Rawls's* *A Theory of Justice*, which defined justice as fairness crucial for a liberal society to function. The publication of John Rawls's text in 1971 saw a growing interest in rights-based political philosophy in universities. At the time, utilitarianism dominated political philosophy; Rawls's text, however, revisited the idea of the "social contract"* between the government and the governed which utilitarianism had displaced. Hundreds of books and thousands of articles have been written in response to Rawls's work—evidence that rights-based political philosophy has by and large displaced the dominance of utilitarianism in political philosophy.

Since the 1950s, scholarship on Mill's *Utilitarianism* has focused on providing a correct interpretation of the text. The body of secondary literature on Mill's work is immense and continues to grow. It is likely that the text's core ideas will be even further developed, since many philosophers are now returning to Mill's ideas about human happiness, the principle of utility,* and the relationship between justice and utility. For the foreseeable future these will remain the main interests of philosophers actively engaging with the text.

Future Directions

Utilitarianism will continue to be developed, we must assume, often in direct dialogue with its fiercest critics. This mirrors the way

Mill developed his own account in direct response to the critics of his day. Although the extent to which Mill's *Utilitarianism* will contribute to these developments is difficult to predict, several contemporary philosophers can be mentioned who show great promise in continuing to build on Mill's text.

The British philosopher Alan Ryan,* for instance, has subjected chapter 5 of the text to close analysis and combined the insights it contains with several chapters from Mill's *On Liberty* and sections of Mill's *A System of Logic*. Ryan concludes that the liberal doctrine that Mill developed is based on utilitarianism, thereby reestablishing a close connection between political liberalism and Mill's classical utilitarianism.[1] Scholars such as Ryan argue that Mill's *Utilitarianism* can better be understood if it is examined in relation to his other works.

The British political philosopher John Gray* and the philosophy scholar Fred Berger,* on the other hand, have examined Mill's central concept of happiness, and tried to show its significance to his understanding of rights, liberty, justice, freedom, and moral rules.[2] The scholar of ethics John Skorupski,* a long-standing admirer of Mill's work, is currently assessing the critique that John Rawls* leveled against Mill's concept of liberty. Ongoing research such as this might pave the way for a return of Mill's liberalism to the philosophical and political forefront.

These examples demonstrate that *Utilitarianism* is by no means an ornament in the history of outdated ideas. It continues to be a source of inspiration for moral philosophers who are utilitarians and a challenge for those who are not.

Summary

John Stuart Mill's *Utilitarianism* is a key work in the history of moral philosophy. It contains a systematic and thorough answer to the question, "How should we live our lives and how should we live together?"

Mill combines the insights of his father James Mill* and his tutor Jeremy Bentham,* together with ethical insights from ancient philosophers. He argues that happiness is the ultimate goal of human life, so that an action is right if it tends to increase the amount of human happiness and reduce the amount of unhappiness in the world. The appeal of Mill's account of utilitarianism stems from his effort to prove this principle of utility on an empirical* basis, by drawing a distinction between higher and lower pleasures, and by developing a utility-based view of justice.

Although Mill's work was heavily criticized at the time, it has had, and continues to have, a great impact on moral philosophy. Later developments of utilitarianism have built on Mill's insight and have often drawn inspiration from his text. Scholars also continue to investigate the central arguments of *Utilitarianism* in an attempt to show that the many criticisms it has faced are based on misinterpretations.

For anyone with an interest in questions about how to live a good life and how to act well in this world, *Utilitarianism* remains one of the most important texts to study.

NOTES

1   Alan Ryan, "John Stuart Mill and the Art of Living," in *J. S. Mill's "On Liberty" in Focus*, eds. John Gray and G. W. Smith (London: Routledge, 1991); John Rees, *John Stuart Mill's "On Liberty"* (Oxford: Clarendon Press, 1985); Fred Berger, *Happiness, Justice and Freedom: The Moral and Political Philosophy of John Stuart Mill* (Berkeley: University of California Press, 1984).

2   John Gray, *Mill on Liberty: A Defence* (London: Routledge & Kegan Paul, 1983); Berger, *Happiness, Justice and Freedom*.

GLOSSARIES

GLOSSARY OF TERMS

A priori: the kind of knowledge that we can acquire independently of experience, such as mathematical knowledge.

Act utilitarianism: a moral theory stating that the moral goodness of an action depends on the degree to which *that action* affects the total amount of happiness.

Calculative: based on calculation.

Deontology: an approach to ethics founded on notions of duty and moral obligation that owes much to the eighteenth-century German philosopher Immanuel Kant.

Emancipation: being set free from legal, social, or political restrictions.

Empirical: based on experience, normally sensory experience.

Empiricism: the philosophical view that all knowledge is based on sense experience, as opposed to reason or intuition.

Ethical intuitionism: a doctrine that states that we have *a priori* knowledge of moral truths. Morality is known through intuition; intuition relates to direct awareness of certain objects.

Ethical theory: a reasoned account of how humans ought to behave or act.

Fallacy: a fault in reasoning that makes an argument or statement invalid.

Fallacy of composition: a false inference that arises when one infers that what is true of a part (or parts) is true of the whole. For example: all the parts of a bicycle are light, therefore a bicycle is light.

French Revolution: between 1789 and 1799, France experienced turmoil and a revolution that saw the end of the monarchy and the execution of King Louis XVI in 1793. Prior to the revolution, church leaders and the ruling classes wielded considerable power and led privileged lives while ordinary people faced poverty and high taxes.

Greatest happiness principle: the ethical *principle* that an action is right in so far as it promotes the *greatest happiness* of the *greatest* number of those affected.

Hedonism: a doctrine that states that happiness or pleasure is the ultimate good.

Hedonistic: relying on the experience of pleasure.

Idealism: a philosophical doctrine that asserts that reality is made up of ideas, minds, or thoughts, not physical objects. Importantly, however, the term does not have a single meaning. In Britain, idealism was a dominant philosophical movement from the mid-nineteenth to the early twentieth century.

Inductive school of ethics: a school of philosophy that claims that moral knowledge is based on observation and experience.

Industrial Revolution: the period from the eighteenth to the nineteenth century when Britain experienced fundamental economic, social, and technological change as the nation moved to an economy based on industrial production.

Intuitionism: the belief that all knowledge is based on intuition— that is, that knowledge is acquired without appeal to reason, observation, or experience.

Intuitive school of ethics: a school of thought that points to the existence of moral intuition or sense. For such a school, general moral principles are known *a priori*; that is, they are self-evident.

Jurist: a legal scholar or legal theorist, studying theories of law.

Kantian deontology: a theory in moral philosophy that centers on duties and rules. Kant's version of deontology states that we must act for the sake of duty alone, by which he means that we must act in line with the moral law.

Liberalism: a political movement that defended individual freedom against unlimited state control.

Logical fallacy: a fault in reasoning that makes an argument or statement invalid.

Logical positivism: a theory of knowledge according to which cognitively meaningful statements are those that can be empirically verified or logically inferred from empirically verifiable statements.

Moral obligation: something one must do or has a duty to do independent of personal or circumstantial factors; "Do not kill," for example.

Normative: relating to an ideal standard or model, or being based on what is considered to be the normal or correct way of doing something.

Philosophical radicals: a group of utilitarian thinkers who demanded social reform in England.

Positivism: the belief that scientific knowledge must be based directly or indirectly on sensory experience and tested via experiments.

Preference utilitarianism: a moral theory stating that the goodness of an action depends on whether it promotes people in being able to satisfy their own desires and preferences.

Principle of utility: this states that actions or behaviors are right in so far as they promote happiness or pleasure, or wrong if they tend to produce unhappiness or pain.

Romanticism: a nineteenth-century philosophical, artistic, and literary movement, prevalent in Germany, which valued non-rational aspects of human nature such as imagination and feelings.

Rule utilitarianism: a moral theory stating that the moral goodness of an action depends on whether it fits rules that normally result in a positive effect on the total amount of happiness.

Social contract: the idea that legitimate state authority must stem from the consent of the governed.

Tabula rasa: a Latin phrase, often translated as "blank slate." In philosophy it is used to describe the idea that people are born without mental content and innate knowledge, and that all knowledge comes from experience and perception. The philosophical idea of *tabula rasa* originated from John Locke.

Two-level utilitarianism: a position in moral philosophy stating that we should follow rules based on the principle of utility, but in exceptional circumstances break those rules. These exceptional circumstances are when following a rule will result in a diminution of the total amount of happiness.

Virtue ethics: a label given to the ethical views of the Ancient Greeks, whereby the cultivation of virtues of excellences of character was deemed central.

PEOPLE MENTIONED IN THE TEXT

Aristippus (435–356 B.C.E.) was an Ancient Greek ethical thinker who founded the Cyrenaic school of philosophy. A pupil of Socrates, he taught that the goal of life was to seek pleasure by maintaining control over adversity and prosperity.

Aristotle (384–322 B.C.E.) was a student of Plato and classical Greek philosopher whose ideas have shaped Western philosophy. His work covers a variety of subjects, including linguistics, physics, poetry, music, biology, politics, and ethics.

Alexander Bain (1818–1903) was a Scottish philosopher and educationalist who played a significant role in the development of modern psychology. He was also a radical follower of John Stuart Mill. One of his major works is *The Emotions and the Will* (1859).

Cesare Beccaria (1738–94) was an Italian philosopher, politician, and jurist. He is best known for his work *On Crimes and Punishments* (1674), which was critical of the death penalty and torture.

Jeremy Bentham (1748–1832) is regarded as the father of modern utilitarianism. He was a social reformer, philosopher, and jurist who advocated a criminal justice system and state institutions that produce "the greatest happiness of the greatest number."

Fred Berger (1937–1986) was a professor of philosophy at the University of California, Davis. He wrote mainly on ethics and legal philosophy.

Francis H. Bradley (1846–1924) was a British philosopher who was best known for his work *Appearance and Reality: A Metaphysical Essay* (1893).

Thomas Carlyle (1795–1881) was a Scottish historian and philosopher, and one of the prominent literary figures of his time.

Samuel Taylor Coleridge (1772–1834) was a leading English Romantic poet.

Auguste Comte (1798–1857) was a French philosopher and social theorist who coined the term "sociology." He also developed the doctrine of positivism.

Roger Crisp (b. 1961) is Professor of Moral Philosophy and Uehiro Fellow and Tutor in Philosophy at St. Anne's College, Oxford. His work is primarily concerned with ethics.

Epicurus (341–270 B.C.E.) was a classical Greek philosopher known for advancing Epicureanism—a school of philosophy that advocated the pursuit of pleasure, particularly mental pleasure, which it considered the highest good.

Philippa Foot (1920–2010) was a British philosopher best known for her work in ethics, especially for her effort at revitalizing ancient virtue ethics. Her best-known works are *Virtues and Vices and Other Essays in Moral Philosophy* (1978) and *Natural Goodness* (2001).

John Gray (b. 1948) is an English political philosopher. The author of several best-selling works dealing with philosophical issues, he is noted for his work in analytic philosophy and the history of ideas.

Thomas Hill Green (1836–82) was a distinguished and influential British philosopher and political theorist.

Richard Mervyn Hare (1919–2002) was a British philosopher at Oxford University specializing in metaethics. His best-known works are *The Language of Morals* (1952), *Freedom and Reason* (1963), and *Moral Thinking* (1981), in which he defends the view known as "Universal Prescriptivism."

John Harsanyi (1920–2000) was an American Hungarian economist and Nobel prize winner, best known for his work in game theory.

Claude Adrien Helvétius (1715–71) was a French philosopher and philanthropist who advocated a materialist theory of human nature. This theory states that our actions are determined by our surroundings.

David Hume (1711–76) was a Scottish philosopher, economist, and historian best known for his empiricism (the idea that all knowledge arises from the senses) and skepticism (the philosophical position that true knowledge is completely unattainable).

Francis Hutcheson (1694–1746) was an Irish-born Scottish philosopher and Professor of Moral Philosophy at the University of Glasgow. He is best known for defending the moral sense theory and moral sentimentalism, a theory that states that humans have a moral sense through which they can approve or disapprove of human action.

Immanuel Kant (1724–1804) was a key eighteenth-century German philosopher who played a significant role in the development of modern philosophy. He is known for one of the most influential works in philosophy, the *Critique of Pure Reason* (1781), and for *Groundwork of the Metaphysics of Morals* (1785).

Christine Korsgaard (b. 1952) is a professor of philosophy at Harvard University, specializing in moral philosophy. She is best known for her work on Kant and Aristotle, and for her critique of utilitarianism.

William E. H. Lecky (1838–1903) was an Irish historian and political theorist, best known for his *A History of the Rise and Influence of Rationalism in Europe* (1865) and *A History of European Morals from Augustus to Charlemagne* (1869).

John Locke (1632–1704) was a British philosopher, medical researcher, and academic. He is known as the father of classical liberalism.

David Lyons (b. 1935) is a professor of law and professor of philosophy at Boston University, specializing in ethics and jurisprudence.

Harriet Taylor Mill (1807–58) was a British philosopher and campaigner for women's rights who made significant contributions to the utilitarian movement.

James Mill (1773–1836) was a Scottish philosopher, historian, and economist who was prominent as a representative of the utilitarian school of thought. He wrote a number of articles on various subjects, including education, government, prisons, and colonies. One of his leading texts is *Elements of Political Economy* (1821). He was the father of John Stuart Mill.

George Edward Moore (1873–1958) was an influential British philosopher, best known for his *Principia Ethica*, first published in 1903.

Robert Nozick (1938–2002) was one of the most influential political philosophers of the late twentieth century, best known for his *Anarchy, State, and Utopia* (1974).

Plato (427–347 B.C.E.) was one of the best-known and most influential classical Greek philosophers. His text *The Republic*, which focuses on issues such as society, justice, and the individual, is considered to be one of the greatest philosophical texts ever written.

John Rawls (1921–2002) was an American political philosopher who was one of the leading thinkers in twentieth-century political philosophy and a strong advocate of individual rights. He is best known for his *A Theory of Justice* (1971), a landmark book of the twentieth century.

David Ricardo (1772–1823) was a British political economist whose writings made significant contributions to labor markets and international trade.

Jonathan Riley is a professor of philosophy and political economy at Tulane University, United States, specializing in utilitarianism, especially the philosophy of John Stuart Mill.

John Ruskin (1819–1900) is regarded as one of the greatest social commentators and art critics of the Victorian era.

Alan Ryan (b. 1940) is a British political philosopher and professor emeritus of political theory at the University of Oxford. He has written extensively on John Stuart Mill.

Jerome B. Schneewind (b. 1930) is an American academic and philosopher who is currently a professor emeritus of philosophy at Johns Hopkins University in Maryland.

James Seth (1860–1925) was a Scottish philosopher who held a chair in moral philosophy at Edinburgh University for 26 years.

Peter Singer (b. 1946) is an Australian moral philosopher affiliated with Princeton University and the University of Melbourne. He specializes in applied ethics, defending preference utilitarianism, and is best known for his *Animal Liberation* (1975) and his highly controversial support of infanticide.

John Skorupski (b. 1946) is a professor emeritus of moral philosophy at the University of St. Andrews, specializing in ethics, epistemology, and moral philosophy, and best known for his *The Domain of Reasons* (2010).

Socrates (470–390 B.C.E.) was the classical Greek philosopher who founded Western philosophy, and whose ideas were passed on to us primarily by his disciple Plato.

James Opie Urmson (1915–2012) was a philosopher and classicist who spent most of his professional career at the University of Oxford, specializing in ethics, ancient philosophy, and the work of George Berkeley.

Carl Wellman is a professor emeritus of philosophy, and Hortense and Tobias Lewin Distinguished University Professor in the Humanities at Washington University in St. Louis, specializing in ethics and philosophy of law.

Henry R. West is a professor emeritus of philosophy at Macalester College, Minnesota, specializing in utilitarianism, especially the philosophy of John Stuart Mill.

William Whewell (1794–1866) was a British philosopher, scientist, and theologian who was opposed to empiricism.

Bernard Williams (1929–2003) was a British moral philosopher at Cambridge University, and is considered to be one of the greatest British philosophers of the twentieth century.

William Wordsworth (1770–1850) was a leading English Romantic poet.

WORKS CITED

WORKS CITED

Aristotle. *Nicomachean Ethics*. In *The Complete Works of Aristotle, The Revised Oxford Translation*, edited by Jonathan Barnes. Princeton, NJ: Princeton University Press, 1995.

Bentham, Jeremy. *An Introduction to the Principles of Morals and Legislation*. Edited by J. H. Burns and H. L. A. Hurt. London: Athlone, 1970.

Berger, Fred. *Happiness, Justice and Freedom: The Moral and Political Philosophy of John Stuart Mill*. Berkeley: University of California Press, 1984.

Bradley, Francis Herbert. *Ethical Studies*. London: Oxford University Press, 1962.

Brown, Campbell. "Consequentialise This." *Ethics* 121, no. 4 (2011): 749–71.

Crisp, Roger. "Introduction." In *Utilitarianism*, by John Stuart Mill, edited by Roger Crisp, 5–32. Oxford: Oxford University Press, 1998.

———. *Routledge Philosophy Guidebook to Mill on Utilitarianism*. London: Routledge, 1977.

Devigne, Robert. *Reforming Liberalism: J. S. Mill's Use of Ancient, Religious, Liberal, and Romantic Moralities*. New Haven, CT: Yale University Press, 2006.

Foot, Philippa. "The Problem of Abortion and the Doctrine of the Double Effect." In *Virtues and Vices*. Oxford: Basil Blackwell, 1978.

Gray, John. *Mill on Liberty: A Defence*. London: Routledge & Kegal Paul, 1983.

Green, Thomas Hill. *Prolegomena to Ethics*. Edited by David O. Brink. Oxford: Clarendon Press, 2003.

Hare, R. M. "Principles." *Proceedings of the Aristotelian Society, New Series* 73 (1972–73): 1–18.

Harsanyi, John. "Morality and the Theory of Rational Behaviour." In *Utilitarianism and Beyond*, edited by Amartya Sen and Bernard Williams, 39–62. Cambridge: Cambridge University Press, 1982.

Kant, Immanuel. *Groundwork of the Metaphysics of Morals*. Edited and translated by Mary J. Gregor. Cambridge: Cambridge University Press, [1785] 1998.

Korsgaard, Christine. "On Having a Good." *Philosophy: The Journal of the Royal Institute of Philosophy* 89, no. 3 (2014): 405–29.

Mill, John Stuart. "Bentham." In *Utilitarianism and Other Essays*, edited by Alan Ryan, 132–76. London: Penguin Books, 2004.

— — —. "Coleridge." In *Utilitarianism and Other Essays*, edited by Alan Ryan, 177–226. London: Penguin Books, 2004.

— — —. *A System of Logic, Ratiocinative and Inductive: Being a Connected View of the Principles of Evidence and the Methods of Scientific Investigation*. Edited by J. M. Robson. Toronto: University of Toronto Press, 1973.

— — —. *Autobiography*. Edited with an introduction and notes by Jack Stillinger. London: Oxford University Press, 1971.

— — —. *Considerations on Representative Government*. London: Longmans, Green & Co., 1888.

— — —. *On Liberty*. London: Penguin, 2010.

— — —. *Principles of Political Economy: With Some of their Applications to Social Philosophy*. London: Longmans, Green & Co., 1911.

— — —. *The Letters of John Stuart Mill*, vol. 2. Edited with an introduction by Hugh S. R. Elliot, with a note on Mill's private life by Mary Taylor. New York: Longmans, Green & Co., 1910.

— — —. *The Subjection of Women*. London: Longmans, Green & Co., 1883.

— — —. *Utilitarianism*. Edited by Roger Crisp. Oxford: Oxford University Press, 1998.

Miller, Dale E., *John Stuart Mill: Moral, Social and Political Thought*. Cambridge: Cambridge University Press, 2010.

Moore, G. E. *Principia Ethica*. Cambridge: Cambridge University Press, 1993.

Nozick, Robert. *Anarchy, State, and Utopia.* Oxford: Blackwell, 1974.

Rawls, John. *A Theory of Justice*. Delhi: Belknap Press of Harvard University, 1971.

Rees, John. *John Stuart Mill's "On Liberty"*. Oxford: Clarendon Press, 1985.

Riley, Jonathan. "Mill's Extraordinary Moral Theory." *Politics, Philosophy and Economics* 9, no. 1 (2010): 67–116.

Rosen, Fred. *Classical Utilitarianism from Hume to Mill.* London: Routledge, 2003.

Ryan, Alan. "Introduction." In *Utilitarianism and Other Essays*, by John Stuart Mill, edited by Alan Ryan, 7–63. London: Penguin Books, 2004.

— — —. *John Stuart Mill*. London: Routledge & Kegan Paul, 1974.

— — —. "John Stuart Mill and the Art of Living." In *J. S. Mill's "On Liberty" in Focus*, edited by John Gray and G. W. Smith, 162–8. London: Routledge, 1991.

— — —. *On Politics: A History of Political Thought from Herodotus to the Present*. London: Allen Lane, 2012.

Schneewind, J. B. "Concerning Some Criticisms of Mill's *Utilitarianism*, 1861–76." In *James and John Stuart Mill: Papers of the Centenary Conference*, edited by John M. Robson and Michael Laine, 35–54. Toronto and Buffalo: University of Toronto Press, 1976.

Seth, James. "The Alleged Fallacies in Mill's 'Utilitarianism'." *The Philosophical Review* 17, no. 5 (1908): 469–88.

Singer, Peter. *Practical Ethics.* Cambridge: Cambridge University Press, 1979.

Skorpuski, John. "Introduction." In *Cambridge Companion to Mill*, edited by John Skorupski, 1–34. Cambridge, Cambridge University Press, 1998.

Smart, J. J. C. *and Bernard Williams. Utilitarianism: For and Against*. Cambridge: Cambridge University Press, 1973.

Urmson, J. O. "The Interpretation of the Moral Philosophy of J. S. Mill." *The Philosophical Quarterly* 3 (1953): 33–9.

West, Henry R. *An Introduction to Mill's Ethics*. Cambridge: Cambridge University Press, 2004.

THE MACAT LIBRARY
BY DISCIPLINE

AFRICANA STUDIES

Chinua Achebe's *An Image of Africa: Racism in Conrad's Heart of Darkness*
W. E. B. Du Bois's *The Souls of Black Folk*
Zora Neale Huston's *Characteristics of Negro Expression*
Martin Luther King Jr's *Why We Can't Wait*
Toni Morrison's *Playing in the Dark: Whiteness in the American Literary Imagination*

ANTHROPOLOGY

Arjun Appadurai's *Modernity at Large: Cultural Dimensions of Globalisation*
Philippe Ariès's *Centuries of Childhood*
Franz Boas's *Race, Language and Culture*
Kim Chan & Renée Mauborgne's *Blue Ocean Strategy*
Jared Diamond's *Guns, Germs & Steel: the Fate of Human Societies*
Jared Diamond's *Collapse: How Societies Choose to Fail or Survive*
E. E. Evans-Pritchard's *Witchcraft, Oracles and Magic Among the Azande*
James Ferguson's *The Anti-Politics Machine*
Clifford Geertz's *The Interpretation of Cultures*
David Graeber's *Debt: the First 5000 Years*
Karen Ho's *Liquidated: An Ethnography of Wall Street*
Geert Hofstede's *Culture's Consequences: Comparing Values, Behaviors, Institutes and Organizations across Nations*
Claude Lévi-Strauss's *Structural Anthropology*
Jay Macleod's *Ain't No Makin' It: Aspirations and Attainment in a Low-Income Neighborhood*
Saba Mahmood's *The Politics of Piety: The Islamic Revival and the Feminist Subjec*t
Marcel Mauss's *The Gift*

BUSINESS

Jean Lave & Etienne Wenger's *Situated Learning*
Theodore Levitt's *Marketing Myopia*
Burton G. Malkiel's *A Random Walk Down Wall Street*
Douglas McGregor's *The Human Side of Enterprise*
Michael Porter's *Competitive Strategy: Creating and Sustaining Superior Performance*
John Kotter's *Leading Change*
C. K. Prahalad & Gary Hamel's *The Core Competence of the Corporation*

CRIMINOLOGY

Michelle Alexander's *The New Jim Crow: Mass Incarceration in the Age of Colorblindness*
Michael R. Gottfredson & Travis Hirschi's *A General Theory of Crime*
Richard Herrnstein & Charles A. Murray's *The Bell Curve: Intelligence and Class Structure in American Life*
Elizabeth Loftus's *Eyewitness Testimony*
Jay Macleod's *Ain't No Makin' It: Aspirations and Attainment in a Low-Income Neighborhood*
Philip Zimbardo's *The Lucifer Effect*

ECONOMICS

Janet Abu-Lughod's *Before European Hegemony*
Ha-Joon Chang's *Kicking Away the Ladder*
David Brion Davis's *The Problem of Slavery in the Age of Revolution*
Milton Friedman's *The Role of Monetary Policy*
Milton Friedman's *Capitalism and Freedom*
David Graeber's *Debt: the First 5000 Years*
Friedrich Hayek's *The Road to Serfdom*
Karen Ho's *Liquidated: An Ethnography of Wall Street*

John Maynard Keynes's *The General Theory of Employment, Interest and Money*
Charles P. Kindleberger's *Manias, Panics and Crashes*
Robert Lucas's *Why Doesn't Capital Flow from Rich to Poor Countries?*
Burton G. Malkiel's *A Random Walk Down Wall Street*
Thomas Robert Malthus's *An Essay on the Principle of Population*
Karl Marx's *Capital*
Thomas Piketty's *Capital in the Twenty-First Century*
Amartya Sen's *Development as Freedom*
Adam Smith's *The Wealth of Nations*
Nassim Nicholas Taleb's *The Black Swan: The Impact of the Highly Improbable*
Amos Tversky's & Daniel Kahneman's *Judgment under Uncertainty: Heuristics and Biases*
Mahbub Ul Haq's *Reflections on Human Development*
Max Weber's *The Protestant Ethic and the Spirit of Capitalism*

FEMINISM AND GENDER STUDIES

Judith Butler's *Gender Trouble*
Simone De Beauvoir's *The Second Sex*
Michel Foucault's *History of Sexuality*
Betty Friedan's *The Feminine Mystique*
Saba Mahmood's *The Politics of Piety: The Islamic Revival and the Feminist Subject*
Joan Wallach Scott's *Gender and the Politics of History*
Mary Wollstonecraft's *A Vindication of the Rights of Women*
Virginia Woolf's *A Room of One's Own*

GEOGRAPHY

The Brundtland Report's *Our Common Future*
Rachel Carson's *Silent Spring*
Charles Darwin's *On the Origin of Species*
James Ferguson's *The Anti-Politics Machine*
Jane Jacobs's *The Death and Life of Great American Cities*
James Lovelock's *Gaia: A New Look at Life on Earth*
Amartya Sen's *Development as Freedom*
Mathis Wackernagel & William Rees's *Our Ecological Footprint*

HISTORY

Janet Abu-Lughod's *Before European Hegemony*
Benedict Anderson's *Imagined Communities*
Bernard Bailyn's *The Ideological Origins of the American Revolution*
Hanna Batatu's *The Old Social Classes And The Revolutionary Movements Of Iraq*
Christopher Browning's *Ordinary Men: Reserve Police Batallion 101 and the Final Solution in Poland*
Edmund Burke's *Reflections on the Revolution in France*
William Cronon's *Nature's Metropolis: Chicago And The Great West*
Alfred W. Crosby's *The Columbian Exchange*
Hamid Dabashi's *Iran: A People Interrupted*
David Brion Davis's *The Problem of Slavery in the Age of Revolution*
Nathalie Zemon Davis's *The Return of Martin Guerre*
Jared Diamond's *Guns, Germs & Steel: the Fate of Human Societies*
Frank Dikotter's *Mao's Great Famine*
John W Dower's *War Without Mercy: Race And Power In The Pacific War*
W. E. B. Du Bois's *The Souls of Black Folk*
Richard J. Evans's *In Defence of History*
Lucien Febvre's *The Problem of Unbelief in the 16th Century*
Sheila Fitzpatrick's *Everyday Stalinism*

Eric Foner's *Reconstruction: America's Unfinished Revolution, 1863-1877*
Michel Foucault's *Discipline and Punish*
Michel Foucault's *History of Sexuality*
Francis Fukuyama's *The End of History and the Last Man*
John Lewis Gaddis's *We Now Know: Rethinking Cold War History*
Ernest Gellner's *Nations and Nationalism*
Eugene Genovese's *Roll, Jordan, Roll: The World the Slaves Made*
Carlo Ginzburg's *The Night Battles*
Daniel Goldhagen's *Hitler's Willing Executioners*
Jack Goldstone's *Revolution and Rebellion in the Early Modern World*
Antonio Gramsci's *The Prison Notebooks*
Alexander Hamilton, John Jay & James Madison's *The Federalist Papers*
Christopher Hill's *The World Turned Upside Down*
Carole Hillenbrand's *The Crusades: Islamic Perspectives*
Thomas Hobbes's *Leviathan*
Eric Hobsbawm's *The Age Of Revolution*
John A. Hobson's *Imperialism: A Study*
Albert Hourani's *History of the Arab Peoples*
Samuel P. Huntington's *The Clash of Civilizations and the Remaking of World Order*
C. L. R. James's *The Black Jacobins*
Tony Judt's *Postwar: A History of Europe Since 1945*
Ernst Kantorowicz's *The King's Two Bodies: A Study in Medieval Political Theology*
Paul Kennedy's *The Rise and Fall of the Great Powers*
Ian Kershaw's *The "Hitler Myth": Image and Reality in the Third Reich*
John Maynard Keynes's *The General Theory of Employment, Interest and Money*
Charles P. Kindleberger's *Manias, Panics and Crashes*
Martin Luther King Jr's *Why We Can't Wait*
Henry Kissinger's *World Order: Reflections on the Character of Nations and the Course of History*
Thomas Kuhn's *The Structure of Scientific Revolutions*
Georges Lefebvre's *The Coming of the French Revolution*
John Locke's *Two Treatises of Government*
Niccolò Machiavelli's *The Prince*
Thomas Robert Malthus's *An Essay on the Principle of Population*
Mahmood Mamdani's *Citizen and Subject: Contemporary Africa And The Legacy Of Late Colonialism*
Karl Marx's *Capital*
Stanley Milgram's *Obedience to Authority*
John Stuart Mill's *On Liberty*
Thomas Paine's *Common Sense*
Thomas Paine's *Rights of Man*
Geoffrey Parker's *Global Crisis: War, Climate Change and Catastrophe in the Seventeenth Century*
Jonathan Riley-Smith's *The First Crusade and the Idea of Crusading*
Jean-Jacques Rousseau's *The Social Contract*
Joan Wallach Scott's *Gender and the Politics of History*
Theda Skocpol's *States and Social Revolutions*
Adam Smith's *The Wealth of Nations*
Timothy Snyder's *Bloodlands: Europe Between Hitler and Stalin*
Sun Tzu's *The Art of War*
Keith Thomas's *Religion and the Decline of Magic*
Thucydides's *The History of the Peloponnesian War*
Frederick Jackson Turner's *The Significance of the Frontier in American History*
Odd Arne Westad's *The Global Cold War: Third World Interventions And The Making Of Our Times*

LITERATURE

Chinua Achebe's *An Image of Africa: Racism in Conrad's Heart of Darkness*
Roland Barthes's *Mythologies*
Homi K. Bhabha's *The Location of Culture*
Judith Butler's *Gender Trouble*
Simone De Beauvoir's *The Second Sex*
Ferdinand De Saussure's *Course in General Linguistics*
T. S. Eliot's *The Sacred Wood: Essays on Poetry and Criticism*
Zora Neale Huston's *Characteristics of Negro Expression*
Toni Morrison's *Playing in the Dark: Whiteness in the American Literary Imagination*
Edward Said's *Orientalism*
Gayatri Chakravorty Spivak's *Can the Subaltern Speak?*
Mary Wollstonecraft's *A Vindication of the Rights of Women*
Virginia Woolf's *A Room of One's Own*

PHILOSOPHY

Elizabeth Anscombe's *Modern Moral Philosophy*
Hannah Arendt's *The Human Condition*
Aristotle's *Metaphysics*
Aristotle's *Nicomachean Ethics*
Edmund Gettier's *Is Justified True Belief Knowledge?*
Georg Wilhelm Friedrich Hegel's *Phenomenology of Spirit*
David Hume's *Dialogues Concerning Natural Religion*
David Hume's *The Enquiry for Human Understanding*
Immanuel Kant's *Religion within the Boundaries of Mere Reason*
Immanuel Kant's *Critique of Pure Reason*
Søren Kierkegaard's *The Sickness Unto Death*
Søren Kierkegaard's *Fear and Trembling*
C. S. Lewis's *The Abolition of Man*
Alasdair MacIntyre's *After Virtue*
Marcus Aurelius's *Meditations*
Friedrich Nietzsche's *On the Genealogy of Morality*
Friedrich Nietzsche's *Beyond Good and Evil*
Plato's *Republic*
Plato's *Symposium*
Jean-Jacques Rousseau's *The Social Contract*
Gilbert Ryle's *The Concept of Mind*
Baruch Spinoza's *Ethics*
Sun Tzu's *The Art of War*
Ludwig Wittgenstein's *Philosophical Investigations*

POLITICS

Benedict Anderson's *Imagined Communities*
Aristotle's *Politics*
Bernard Bailyn's *The Ideological Origins of the American Revolution*
Edmund Burke's *Reflections on the Revolution in France*
John C. Calhoun's *A Disquisition on Government*
Ha-Joon Chang's *Kicking Away the Ladder*
Hamid Dabashi's *Iran: A People Interrupted*
Hamid Dabashi's *Theology of Discontent: The Ideological Foundation of the Islamic Revolution in Iran*
Robert Dahl's *Democracy and its Critics*
Robert Dahl's *Who Governs?*
David Brion Davis's *The Problem of Slavery in the Age of Revolution*

Alexis De Tocqueville's *Democracy in America*
James Ferguson's *The Anti-Politics Machine*
Frank Dikotter's *Mao's Great Famine*
Sheila Fitzpatrick's *Everyday Stalinism*
Eric Foner's *Reconstruction: America's Unfinished Revolution, 1863-1877*
Milton Friedman's *Capitalism and Freedom*
Francis Fukuyama's *The End of History and the Last Man*
John Lewis Gaddis's *We Now Know: Rethinking Cold War History*
Ernest Gellner's *Nations and Nationalism*
David Graeber's *Debt: the First 5000 Years*
Antonio Gramsci's *The Prison Notebooks*
Alexander Hamilton, John Jay & James Madison's *The Federalist Papers*
Friedrich Hayek's *The Road to Serfdom*
Christopher Hill's *The World Turned Upside Down*
Thomas Hobbes's *Leviathan*
John A. Hobson's *Imperialism: A Study*
Samuel P. Huntington's *The Clash of Civilizations and the Remaking of World Order*
Tony Judt's *Postwar: A History of Europe Since 1945*
David C. Kang's *China Rising: Peace, Power and Order in East Asia*
Paul Kennedy's *The Rise and Fall of Great Powers*
Robert Keohane's *After Hegemony*
Martin Luther King Jr.'s *Why We Can't Wait*
Henry Kissinger's *World Order: Reflections on the Character of Nations and the Course of History*
John Locke's *Two Treatises of Government*
Niccolò Machiavelli's *The Prince*
Thomas Robert Malthus's *An Essay on the Principle of Population*
Mahmood Mamdani's *Citizen and Subject: Contemporary Africa And The Legacy Of Late Colonialism*
Karl Marx's *Capital*
John Stuart Mill's *On Liberty*
John Stuart Mill's *Utilitarianism*
Hans Morgenthau's *Politics Among Nations*
Thomas Paine's *Common Sense*
Thomas Paine's *Rights of Man*
Thomas Piketty's *Capital in the Twenty-First Century*
Robert D. Putman's *Bowling Alone*
John Rawls's *Theory of Justice*
Jean-Jacques Rousseau's *The Social Contract*
Theda Skocpol's *States and Social Revolutions*
Adam Smith's *The Wealth of Nations*
Sun Tzu's *The Art of War*
Henry David Thoreau's *Civil Disobedience*
Thucydides's *The History of the Peloponnesian War*
Kenneth Waltz's *Theory of International Politics*
Max Weber's *Politics as a Vocation*
Odd Arne Westad's *The Global Cold War: Third World Interventions And The Making Of Our Times*

POSTCOLONIAL STUDIES

Roland Barthes's *Mythologies*
Frantz Fanon's *Black Skin, White Masks*
Homi K. Bhabha's *The Location of Culture*
Gustavo Gutiérrez's *A Theology of Liberation*
Edward Said's *Orientalism*
Gayatri Chakravorty Spivak's *Can the Subaltern Speak?*

The Macat Library By Discipline

PSYCHOLOGY

Gordon Allport's *The Nature of Prejudice*
Alan Baddeley & Graham Hitch's *Aggression: A Social Learning Analysis*
Albert Bandura's *Aggression: A Social Learning Analysis*
Leon Festinger's *A Theory of Cognitive Dissonance*
Sigmund Freud's *The Interpretation of Dreams*
Betty Friedan's *The Feminine Mystique*
Michael R. Gottfredson & Travis Hirschi's *A General Theory of Crime*
Eric Hoffer's *The True Believer: Thoughts on the Nature of Mass Movements*
William James's *Principles of Psychology*
Elizabeth Loftus's *Eyewitness Testimony*
A. H. Maslow's *A Theory of Human Motivation*
Stanley Milgram's *Obedience to Authority*
Steven Pinker's *The Better Angels of Our Nature*
Oliver Sacks's *The Man Who Mistook His Wife For a Hat*
Richard Thaler & Cass Sunstein's *Nudge: Improving Decisions About Health, Wealth and Happiness*
Amos Tversky's *Judgment under Uncertainty: Heuristics and Biases*
Philip Zimbardo's *The Lucifer Effect*

SCIENCE

Rachel Carson's *Silent Spring*
William Cronon's *Nature's Metropolis: Chicago And The Great West*
Alfred W. Crosby's *The Columbian Exchange*
Charles Darwin's *On the Origin of Species*
Richard Dawkin's *The Selfish Gene*
Thomas Kuhn's *The Structure of Scientific Revolutions*
Geoffrey Parker's *Global Crisis: War, Climate Change and Catastrophe in the Seventeenth Century*
Mathis Wackernagel & William Rees's *Our Ecological Footprint*

SOCIOLOGY

Michelle Alexander's *The New Jim Crow: Mass Incarceration in the Age of Colorblindness*
Gordon Allport's *The Nature of Prejudice*
Albert Bandura's *Aggression: A Social Learning Analysis*
Hanna Batatu's *The Old Social Classes And The Revolutionary Movements Of Iraq*
Ha-Joon Chang's *Kicking Away the Ladder*
W. E. B. Du Bois's *The Souls of Black Folk*
Émile Durkheim's *On Suicide*
Frantz Fanon's *Black Skin, White Masks*
Frantz Fanon's *The Wretched of the Earth*
Eric Foner's *Reconstruction: America's Unfinished Revolution, 1863-1877*
Eugene Genovese's *Roll, Jordan, Roll: The World the Slaves Made*
Jack Goldstone's *Revolution and Rebellion in the Early Modern World*
Antonio Gramsci's *The Prison Notebooks*
Richard Herrnstein & Charles A Murray's *The Bell Curve: Intelligence and Class Structure in American Life*
Eric Hoffer's *The True Believer: Thoughts on the Nature of Mass Movements*
Jane Jacobs's *The Death and Life of Great American Cities*
Robert Lucas's *Why Doesn't Capital Flow from Rich to Poor Countries?*
Jay Macleod's *Ain't No Makin' It: Aspirations and Attainment in a Low Income Neighborhood*
Elaine May's *Homeward Bound: American Families in the Cold War Era*
Douglas McGregor's *The Human Side of Enterprise*
C. Wright Mills's *The Sociological Imagination*

Thomas Piketty's *Capital in the Twenty-First Century*
Robert D. Putman's *Bowling Alone*
David Riesman's *The Lonely Crowd: A Study of the Changing American Character*
Edward Said's *Orientalism*
Joan Wallach Scott's *Gender and the Politics of History*
Theda Skocpol's *States and Social Revolutions*
Max Weber's *The Protestant Ethic and the Spirit of Capitalism*

THEOLOGY

Augustine's *Confessions*
Benedict's *Rule of St Benedict*
Gustavo Gutiérrez's *A Theology of Liberation*
Carole Hillenbrand's *The Crusades: Islamic Perspectives*
David Hume's *Dialogues Concerning Natural Religion*
Immanuel Kant's *Religion within the Boundaries of Mere Reason*
Ernst Kantorowicz's *The King's Two Bodies: A Study in Medieval Political Theology*
Søren Kierkegaard's *The Sickness Unto Death*
C. S. Lewis's *The Abolition of Man*
Saba Mahmood's *The Politics of Piety: The Islamic Revival and the Feminist Subject*
Baruch Spinoza's *Ethics*
Keith Thomas's *Religion and the Decline of Magic*

COMING SOON

Chris Argyris's *The Individual and the Organisation*
Seyla Benhabib's *The Rights of Others*
Walter Benjamin's *The Work Of Art in the Age of Mechanical Reproduction*
John Berger's *Ways of Seeing*
Pierre Bourdieu's *Outline of a Theory of Practice*
Mary Douglas's *Purity and Danger*
Roland Dworkin's *Taking Rights Seriously*
James G. March's *Exploration and Exploitation in Organisational Learning*
Ikujiro Nonaka's *A Dynamic Theory of Organizational Knowledge Creation*
Griselda Pollock's *Vision and Difference*
Amartya Sen's *Inequality Re-Examined*
Susan Sontag's *On Photography*
Yasser Tabbaa's *The Transformation of Islamic Art*
Ludwig von Mises's *Theory of Money and Credit*